Finance Basics
secrets

The experts tell all!

About the author

Stuart Warner NLP Practitioner, BSc (Hons), ACA is a Chartered Accountant with almost two decades of experience in finance. He has spent a large proportion of this time training people for recognized professional qualifications and offering related development training to management and staff at all levels. He is a director of Financial Fluency Ltd (www.financial-fluency.co.uk) and also advises the board of one the UK's top accounting institutes. He provides traditional training, facilitated workshops, simulations and e-learning, as well as finance coaching.

Finance Basics
secrets

Collins
A division of HarperCollins*Publishers*
77-85 Fulham Palace Road, London W6 8JB

www.BusinessSecrets.net

First published in Great Britain in 2010 by HarperCollins*Publishers*
Published in Canada by HarperCollins*Canada*. www.harpercollins.ca
Published in Australia by HarperCollins*Australia*. www.harpercollins.com.au
Published in India by HarperCollins*PublishersIndia*. www.harpercollins.co.in

1

Copyright © HarperCollins*Publishers* 2010

Stuart Warner asserts the moral right to be identified as the author of this work.

A catalogue record for this book is available from the British Library.

ISBN 978-0-00-732809-3

Contents

Financial awareness is fundamental to business success

Many business people, professionals and senior executives who may be experts in their field are sometimes less confident in finance. Quite often this is unfounded and can easily be overcome. In the business world the ability to understand finance and communicate financially is essential.

To date, I've spent almost two decades working in finance. I've spent a large proportion of this time teaching others. Early on, I found that learning finance was akin to learning a language. One of my own finance teachers told me, "It's not the numbers, it's the English you'll find hard!" – and my own experience proves that this is certainly true. Accountants will often use several names for the same thing. Where possible I've tried to give alternative explanations when introducing a financial term. The Jargon Buster at the back of the book should also help you get to grips with some key financial terminology.

In this book I've picked 50 **secrets** that will help you get to grips with finance basics. I've divided the **secrets** into seven chapters which cover seven crucial areas every business person should understand.

Introducing business finance. Business owners, managers and employees need to have a basic level of financial awareness to help a business succeed.

Accounting fundamentals. Make sure you know basic financial terminology and concepts. Be familiar with the main financial statements produced by a business.

Making profit. Profit is the raison d'être for most businesses. Knowing how to make and increase profit is one of the key ingredients for business success.

Managing cash. "Profit is sanity but cash is reality." Without cash a business cannot survive for long. Effective cash management will help a business to endure.

Budgeting. Many businessess invest considerable time in budgeting but few do it successfully. Some practical tips can improve the process.

Evaluating business opportunities. Businesses should use established techniques to help decide whether or not to commit time, resources and money on investment opportunities.

Measuring business performance. A successful business can be judged by the size of its market value. Its performance can be measured by using financial ratios.

From students who are interested in business finance to chief executives who want to know more, this book can help you get to grips with finance basics. You'll even find it interesting and it can help you with your future business activities.

Financial knowledge is not just for accountants – it's for everyone!

Introducing business finance

Owners, managers and employees need to be aware of the financial consequences of running their business. In this chapter I'll explain the different types of business entities. I will show you where a business gets its money from and what it does with it. You'll appreciate the need to record, analyse and summarize business transactions. I'll also explain the essential difference between financial accountants and management accountants.

1.1

Know the different business entities

A useful starting point to understanding business finance is to appreciate the different ways of trading. There are three main categories: sole traders, partnerships and limited companies. Each offers advantages and disadvantages in relation to legal issues, taxation and the personal liability of its owners.

1 **Sole traders.** A sole trader or proprietorship is a business with one owner, who has unlimited personal liability. If the business becomes insolvent, the proprietor is personally liable for any unpaid debts. Examples can include shopkeepers, tradesmen (e.g. electricians), hairdressers and florists.

2 **Partnerships.** A partnership is a business with multiple owners, who share profits or losses. The partners can share unlimited personal liability or can take limited liability status. Examples tend to include doctors, dentists, lawyers and accountants.

"A friendship founded on business is better than a business founded on friendship**"** **John D. Rockefeller, industrialist**

3 **Limited companies.** A limited company is a business incorporated by law. Its owners are 'shareholders' who have the benefit of limited liability. If the business becomes insolvent the shareholders are only liable for the amount they invested in the company. Limited liability is a key advantage of turning a business into a limited company and can help to attract potential investors. In practice, however, banks may require personal guarantees from shareholders of small owner-managed businesses for loans or overdrafts. There is also an increased administrative and financial burden, in comparison to sole traders.

A limited company can be 'private' or 'public'. Most companies, especially small ones, are private and are owned by a small number of shareholders. In the UK, private limited company names end with the suffix 'Limited' or 'Ltd'. The directors of a private limited company are also likely to be the majority shareholders.

Public companies are usually much larger than private compacompanies. Their shares can be sold and purchased on a public stock exchange. In the UK public company names end with the suffix 'Public Limited Company' – or 'PLC'.

This book will be useful to all entities and in particular limited companies which experience the most regulation.

Limited liability is a key advantage for limited companies.

1.2

Find out how a business gets money

The majority of businesses need money to get started. The ability to raise finance is essential to the initial and ongoing success of a business. A lack of finance is one of the main ways that businesses fail.

Imagine you about to start a new business that requires $1 million initial investment. Let's say this money is needed for premises, a motor vehicle, computer equipment and goods to sell. If you don't have $1 million, where can you get the money from?

Most entrepreneurs will initially invest their own money when starting a new business. This is known as 'share capital' and for limited companies the owners are called 'shareholders'. 'Share capital' is sometimes referred to as 'equity finance'.

If more money is needed, there are three main options:

1 **Raise further equity finance.** Ask existing shareholders for more money or find investors who wish to become joint owners/shareholders of the business and contribute to the share capital. As these investors will become joint owners of the business, they will have a say in the running of the business. They will also expect returns on their investment in the form of dividends.

"Never spend your money before you have earned it" Thomas Jefferson, 19th-century American President

2 **Borrow money.** Typically from a bank or family and friends. This is known as 'loan finance' or 'debt finance'. It is a common route for shareholders who don't want to share ownership of their business. Equity finance does not have to be repaid, and dividends to shareholders are discretionary. Loan finance, on the other hand, needs to be repaid and will incur interest costs.

3 **Use surplus cash generated from operating activities.** See Secret 4.5 for more on this. The surplus cash must not have been paid as dividends to shareholders or committed elewhere in the business.

There are many other alternative sources of finance for a business. Examples include leasing assets (as opposed to purchasing assets outright), government grants and even sponsorship. Reading a company's financial statements should reveal where they have got their money from (Secret 2.5).

A successful financing strategy is just as important as a successful business strategy.

1.3

Find out how a business uses money

If the first thing a business does is raise finance, the next thing it does is to spend it, usually on assets. These are resources owned or controlled by a business and are used to generate money. Assets are generally the biggest investments made by businesses. Both long-term and short-term assets are essential for most businesses.

There are four main categories of assets, as follows:

1 **Fixed assets.** The term 'fixed assets' refers to assets that are a 'fixed' item within a business, usually for more than a year (and hence long-term assets). Fixed assets are also referred to as 'property, plant and equipment' and sometimes as 'non-current assets'. They are for continuous use in the business and are essentially used to make money. There are many different types of fixed assets found in businesses. The most common types are land, buildings, machinery, fixtures and fittings, office equipment, computers and motor vehicles.

2 **Intangible assets.** Intangible assets are also long-term assets. They are non-physical resources and rights owned by a business that offer a competitive advantage or add value to the business. Examples of intangible assets include brands, trademarks and patents.

3 **Investments.** Many businesses spend their money on investments, which they intend to 'hold' for the future and hence are also long-term assets. Investments include assets such as shares held in other companies and rental property.

4 **Current assets.** The term 'current assets' refers to assets that help on a short-term basis, usually for less than a year. These are assets which are traded e.g. inventory, or by their nature 'liquid', e.g. cash. Money owed by customers is also a current asset because it is a 'future benefit'. The customer will pay cash in the future. Money owed by customers is also referred to as 'debtors', 'accounts receivable', trade receivables' or more simply 'receivables'.

Reading a company's financial statements should reveal what they have spent their money on (Secret 2.5).

Investing money in both long-term and short-term assets is essential for most businesses.

1.4

Appreciate the need for record-keeping

Successful businesses know that accurate record-keeping is not only essential for accounting but also provides information that can be a key source of competitive advantage.

■ **Accounting and bookkeeping.** 'Accounting' can be defined as the provision of financial information concerning the results of a business over a period of time. A business needs to 'account' for what it has done and accounting is a process of recording, analysing and summarizing commercial transactions. The term 'bookkeeping' generally refers to just the recording of transactions.

case study Tom runs a computer services company and understands the benefits of recording, analysing and summarizing all business transactions. The list opposite shows the information about customers that Tom finds useful to record. It is a list that millions of other companies around the world also compile about their customers:

■ **Separate legal entity.** A fundamental principle of accounting is that a business is a separate entity from its owner. For 'limited' companies the concept of separate entity is a legal distinction. As such, business transactions should never be mixed with the personal transactions of the owners, which is also advisable for other business entities. In addition, for 'limited' companies there is a statutory requirement to maintain proper accounting records.

■ **Management and financial accounting.** Once transactions are recorded they need to be analysed and summarized. 'Management accounting' is the use of this data within a business for management information, planning, decision making, and control purposes. 'Financial accounting' is the use of this data to report financial results and the latest position of a business to a number of interested parties, for a number of different purposes. See Secret 1.7 for more detail on the differences between financial and management accounting. See Secret 2.9 for more information on the users of accounts.

■ **Users of financial information.** All users of financial information require quality information which is both relevant and reliable. Therefore it essential that the transactions which underpin this information are properly recorded, analysed and summarized.

Keeping accurate records of business transactions is valuable in many ways.

- Key contact information
- Sales to date
- Forecasted sales
- Credit rating
- Money owed by date
- Distribution costs
- Discounts offered and taken

1.5

Know what a finance department does

A finance department manages the financial operations of a business and provides information and advice to the rest of the business. All areas of a business will have some contact with the finance department. You should understand how a typical finance department operates, and who does what in it.

The four key responsibilities of a finance department are:

■ Ensuring that a business has sufficient money
■ Recording and controlling transactions within a business
■ Providing information internally to managers to help with planning, decision-making and control
■ Reporting information externally to stakeholders such as shareholders and tax authorities

■ **The finance director.** The finance department is usually headed up by a finance director (FD) or chief financial officer (CFO) who, as a board member, is responsible for 'financing and investment strategy' and making sure it supports the 'business strategy'.

"My money goes to my agent, then to my accountant and from him to the tax man" Glenda Jackson, English actress

The FD also runs the finance department, which may include the following roles, depending upon the size and complexity of the business:

■ **The financial controller.** This person has responsibility for recording, analysing and summarizing financial transactions. In particular the financial controller will produce the financial statements. The financial controller may manage a number of accounting staff who look after areas such as sales invoicing; debt collection; purchases; making payments; payroll; fixed assets; and taxation.

■ **The management accountant.** He or she assists management with planning, decision making and control. The management accountant will prepare both regular and ad-hoc reports. These reports will include 'key performance indicators' (KPIs) which measure the performance of individuals, departments and other critical areas of the business. In particular the management accountant will manage the budgeting process.

■ **The treasurer.** Found in larger businesses, the treasurer has responsibility for financing the business and implementing the financing and investment strategy. In particular the treasurer will liaise with banks, manage cash flow and deal with foreign currency exchange.

The finance department is a key function which should contribute to the success of the business.

1.6

Understand the key financial systems

Irrespective of size, businesses need financial systems to record and control business transactions, especially where money comes in or goes out of the business. System controls should prevent, or detect and correct errors as well as minimize the risk of fraud. You need systems for sales, purchases, payroll and, especially, for cash transactions.

■ **Credit sales to customers.** There should be a clear link between credit limits, orders, issues from stock, delivery, invoicing and collecting debts. Supporting documents should be matched at each stage, so customers receive what they order, are correctly invoiced and ultimately pay. The system should keep track of what is owed by each customer and when they are expected to pay.

■ **Non-credit sales to customers.** Non-credit sales will often follow the same system and controls, with instant payment recorded against the invoice.

■ **Cash transactions.** Although the term 'cash' is widely used in finance, very few businesses actually handle cash. Even retailers have a large proportion of customers using payment cards. For many businesses the only cash will be petty cash. Nevertheless, wherever cash is involved, there should be tight controls and links to authorized supporting documents.

■ **Purchases of goods for resale and stock management.** There should be tight controls over purchases, including a clear link to authorized orders and checks that goods or services have actually been received, before any payments are authorized. There should also be links to a stock management system, where applicable. There should be additional controls that purchases are made from approved suppliers at agreed prices. Purchasing systems should monitor payment due dates so businesses can take full advantage of supplier credit.

■ **Payments for expenses and capital expenditure.** The same system and controls will often be used for expenses such as rent and utility bills. High-value capital expenditure will have additional authorization controls.

■ **Payroll.** Payroll is typically the largest and most frequent expense and should have tight controls and segregation of duties. There should be links back to personnel records, authorized pay rates and, where applicable, timesheets. As an additional control the payroll system is often separate to the other systems.

You must record and control business transactions and maintain clear links back to authorized documentation.

1.7

Differentiate financial and management accounting

There are different types of financial information and reports produced by the finance team, which generally fall under two categories: financial accounting and management accounting.

Financial accounts

■ **Purpose.** Financial accounts are used to report the financial results of a business. They are produced at least annually, mainly for the benefit of external users, such as shareholders.

■ **Focus.** The historical financial results of a business.

■ **Scope.** The financial results of the whole business.

■ **Frequency.** Prepared at least annually, although some companies prepare 'interim' financial reports every six months.

■ **Requirement.** Financial accounts are a legal requirement for registered companies.

■ **Format.** There are financial accounting standards which govern the format and contents of financial accounts.

■ **Accuracy.** Financial accounts are required to show a 'true and fair' view. For practical purposes this means that they should be as accurate as possible and not misleading. 'Accuracy' will depend upon the size of a business.

Management accounts

■ **Purpose.** Management accounts provide financial and non-financial information and are used to help managers make informed business decisions. They are usually confidential and not released outside the organization.

■ **Focus.** Use past and present information to make decisions about the future.

■ **Scope.** Can report on products, customers, departments, divisions or the whole business.

■ **Frequency.** Produced whenever required – usually at least monthly.

■ **Requirement.** There are no legal requirements for management accounts. Although, in practice, some external investors, such as banks, may insist on regular management accounts as a condition of funding.

■ **Format.** There are no standard formats or rules for management accounts but some popular established techniques are used, for example, the calculation of profit margins and other financial ratios.

■ **Accuracy.** Management accounts are required to be as accurate as possible as they are used to make critical business decisions. At the same time, as management accounts are used to predict an uncertain future, they can include reasonable approximations.

Financial accounts report historical data. Management accounts help managers make critical decisions.

Accounting fundamentals

You have to walk before you can run. This chapter explains the basic accounting fundamentals which are essential knowledge for anyone in business. The first step is to understand the language of finance used by accountants. Accountancy is notorious for jargon and I will start the chapter by explaining some of the more commonly used terms. I will then move on to some of the most basic financial concepts.

2.1

Make sense of the jargon

Those new to finance can take a while to get used to the terminology used by accountants. Here are some of the common terms used. You can also refer to the 'jargon buster' at the back of the book at any time.

Financial statements and accounting principles

■ **Financial statements.** The collection of formal financial records of a business's activity (namely the balance sheet, income statement, statement of recognized income and expense, and statement of cash flows).

■ **Matching (or accruals) concept.** Costs are accounted for when incurred, and income when earned.

■ **Going concern.** An assumption that the business will continue in operation for the foreseeable future, which provides the basis for the valuation of business assets.

■ **Prudence.** Revenues and profits should only be recognized once their realization is reasonably certain. Conversely, liabilities are accounted for when they are foreseen.

■ **Materiality.** Amount above which an item's omission or mis-statement would affect the view taken by a reasonable user of financial statements.

"People want to learn about finance because they want to know what accountants are talking about" **Anonymous**

Revenue, capital and assets

■ **Asset.** An item of value owned or controlled by a business that will generate a future benefit. Examples include buildings and inventory.

■ **Capital expenditure.** Payments to purchase or improve long-term assets such as property and equipment.

■ **Revenue expenditure.** Expenses incurred in running a business, which do not specifically increase the value of long-term assets.

■ **Receivables (debtors).** Amounts owed by customers paying on credit.

■ **Prepayment.** A payment for goods or services before they have been received. Examples include advance payment of insurance and rent.

Liabilities

■ **Liability.** Money owed by a business. A commitment to transfer economic benefit in the future. Examples include payables and loans.

■ **Payables (or creditors).** Amounts owed to suppliers who have offered credit.

■ **Accrual.** Goods or services received but not yet invoiced by the supplier. Examples include certain goods for resale and utility bills.

■ **Provision.** An amount set aside for a known liability whose extent and timing cannot be precisely determined, e.g. restructuring costs.

■ **Contingent liability.** A liability where the amount and/or likelihood of payment are uncertain. As such, no specific provision is made.

Be aware of common financial terms.

2.2

Discover why timing is essential

The timing of cash receipts and payments may not be the same as the sales and purchases recorded in financial statements. At the end of an accounting period, a business should make sure that everything has been accounted for, when it should be accounted for.

■ **The importance of timing.** Imagine you are shopping in January and make all your purchases using a credit card. Although, you've effectively 'spent' money (or 'incurred' expenditure) in January, you won't actually pay any cash until you pay your credit card bill, perhaps during February. Therefore, the cash cost of the shopping in January is zero.

case study Aaron, a salesperson, would argue that he has made a sale when his customer has placed an order. Helena, a lawyer, would argue that she has made a sale when her client signs a contract. Others may argue it's when goods are delivered, a service is performed, or a customer has paid. However, using the matching concept, Brian, the accountant who works

Now using a business example – imagine a credit sale made in March, where the customer pays in cash during April. Although the business has effectively 'earned' a sale in March, the cash receipts from that customer during March are zero.

These examples highlight the importance of timing in accounting. Expenses can be incurred at different times to the associated cash paid. Likewise, income can be earned at different times to the associated cash received.

■ **The matching (or accruals) concept.** Financial statements 'match' income and expenses to the periods in which they are earned and incurred to show a true and fair view to the users of those statements. This concept is a fundamental accounting concept used by the majority of businesses.

■ **The benefits.** Matching income and expenditure to the periods in which they are earned and incurred enables more accurate and realistic performance measurement. Ultimately this leads to more efficient business management. The timing of cash receipts and payments is still important and businesses will monitor this separately.

Costs are accounted for when incurred and income when earned, as opposed to when cash is received or paid.

for Aaron, Helena and other businesses, only recognizes a sale when it has been 'earned'. Similarly, Brian recognizes a purchase made by Aaron and Helena only when their suppliers have 'earned' the revenue, not when an order is placed, a contract signed, goods received, or a payment made. Revenue and expense recognition is a complex area for Brian.

2.3

Know about double entry bookkeeping

Accountants use an established system of recording financial transactions, called double entry bookkeeping. The globally used system has hardly changed since it was developed in 1494 by Renaissance scholar Luca Pacioli.

Pacioli's principle is that every transaction has a dual effect. For example, if you get paid for work, then the first effect is that you've earned income and the second effect is that you now have more money. If you go clothes shopping, the first effect is that you have more clothes. The second, more unfortunate effect, is that you have less money.

case study Be careful not to confuse the words 'debit' and 'credit'. For Brian and other accountants, a 'debit' represents an asset and a 'credit' a liability. A 'debit' will increase the value of an asset and a 'credit' will reduce its value. For example, a bank receipt, which increases cash (and hence is a business asset) is a debit. Similarly, a bank payment, which reduces cash, is a credit. This is the opposite way around for banks.

"Never call an accountant a credit to his profession; a good account- ant is a debit to his profession"

Sir Charles Lyell, British lawyer and geologist

Likewise, when a business makes a purchase, it (i) incurs an expense and (ii) has less cash. Similarly, when it makes a cash sale it has (i) more income and (ii) more cash. The system is called double entry bookkeeping because every transaction is effectively recorded twice.

■ **Debits and credits.** The two equal and corresponding effects (recordings) of each transaction are termed 'debits' and 'credits'. As this rule is consistently applied, the total amount of debits will always equal the total amount of credits. As such, accounts should always balance.

Don't worry if this appears confusing. Double entry bookkeeping is almost invisible to the owners of many businesses and is something accountants take care of in practice.

Each transaction has a debit and an equal, corresponding credit.

For example: The Little Socks Company has $1,000 in the bank and therefore has an asset of $1,000 which is a 'debit' in The Little Socks accounts. The bank holds the $1,000 but owes it back to The Little Socks, as it is not the bank's money. The bank has a liability to The Little Socks of $1,000 which is therefore a 'credit' in the bank's accounts. The bank tells The Little Socks: "You are in credit for $1,000".

2.4

See how accounting systems work

The key functions of an accountant are to record, analyse and summarize business transactions. Therefore a robust process is needed, and most businesses follow the same established system.

■ **The books of prime entry.** The books of prime entry are used to record all inputs into an accounting system. The key inputs are sales, purchases, cash receipts and cash payments. The term 'cash' is used generically and can represent bank transfers as well as physical cash. The cash books provide an up-to-date record of a business's cash position and should be regularly reconciled with the actual bank account.

case study John works for a pharmaceuticals company that was established in the 1950s. Historically, the company used a manual accounting system, but nowadays, in keeping with most modern businesses, everything is automated, using cost-effective, specialist accounting software. Most of these software packages have inherited terminology from manual

■ The sales and purchase ledgers. The ledgers are a record of how much is owed by customers and owed to suppliers. Every customer has an individual 'account' in the 'sales ledger', against which invoices are issued and payments received are posted. This provides a record of transactions with each customer and the balance owed at a point in time. The 'purchase ledger' works in the same way as the sales ledger and each supplier has a record of invoices received and payments made.

■ The nominal ledger. The books of prime entry feed into the 'nominal ledger' (or 'general ledger'), which is the central accounting record of all business transactions. Each asset or liability and every item of income or expenditure will have its own nominal code, and accountants will be able to extract detailed reports from each code.

■ The financial statements. The financial statements are the collection of formal financial records of a business's activities, namely the balance sheet, the income statement, the statement of recognized income and expense, and the statement of cash flows. Each of the accounts within the nominal ledger are summarized and categorized and filter into the appropriate statement.

Use established accounting systems for bookkeeping.

systems. Whereas the term 'ledger' is still common, the term 'cash' is often interchanged with 'bank'. John's computer systems offer increased control and faster, more detailed reporting. They offer benefits to other areas of the business such as the sales department, which can have access to more accurate and up-to-date customer records.

2.5

Understand the balance sheet

The 'balance sheet' is one of the key financial statements and is a snapshot of the financial position of
a business at a point in time.

■ **What a business owns.** The top half of the balance sheet contains
the different assets a business owns, which are:

■ Long-term (non-current) assets, such as property,
plant and equipment, intangibles and investments.

■ Short-term (current) assets, such as inventory,
money owed by customers and cash.

■ **What a business owes.** The bottom half of the balance sheet
contains the different liabilities a business owes to shareholders and
other third parties, which are:

■ Equity, which consists of share capital and retained
earnings. 'Retained earnings' or 'retained profits' are unspent
or non-distributed profits, which are retained in a business for
future use. They effectively belong to the shareholders and
are therefore a liability of the business.

■ Long-term (non-current) liabilities, such as loans from a bank.

■ Money owed to suppliers and other creditors.

■ Why a balance sheet balances. The top half of a balance sheet will equal the bottom half of a balance sheet due to the principle of double entry bookkeeping – every debit has an equal and opposite credit (Secret 2.3). A business's assets (its debits) will equal its liabilities (its credits). The exact format of the balance sheet will depend upon the type of business and associated accounting conventions.

An illustrative (and simplified) balance sheet is shown below. Presentation may differ according to the type of business and associated accounting conventions.

Example balance sheet at a particular date

	$
Non-current assets	
Property, plant and equipment	150,250
Intangible assets	25,000
Investment property	7,500
Current assets	
Inventories	20,000
Trade and other receivables	18,500
Cash	9,750
TOTAL ASSETS	231,000
Equity	
Share capital	25,000
Retained earnings	97,500
Non-current liabilities	
Bank borrowings	94,250
Current liabilities	
Trade and other payables	14,250
TOTAL EQUITY AND LIABILITIES	231,000

A balance sheet summarizes what a business owns and what it owes.

2.6

Understand the income statement

Whereas the balance sheet is a snapshot of a business at a moment in time, the income statement covers a span of time. It summarizes total income generated and total expenditure incurred over a set period.

Income statements are alternatively referred to as 'profit and loss accounts' and often just 'P&L'. They show whether a business has more income than expenditure (a profit) or vice versa (a loss). The key items within an income statement are outlined below. The terminology depends upon the type of business and associated accounting conventions. See also Secret 2.9 about different accounting regulations.

■ **Revenue.** Alternatively, sales or turnover – the income for a period.
■ **Cost of sales.** The direct cost of sales during a period. This could be the cost of purchases for a retailer or cost of production for a manufacturer. Cost of sales is matched to the sales that took place during the period, as opposed to when the purchase/manufacture took place.
■ **Gross profit.** Revenue less cost of sales – a key performance indicator.
■ **Operating expenses.** The overhead costs of running a business during the period. Examples include distribution, administration and marketing costs.

■ **One-off circumstances.** A business may incur a large and unusual expense or dispose of/close a substantial part of their operations. Depending upon the accounting convention this can be separately disclosed on the income statement or in the supporting notes.

■ **Operating profit.** Or 'results from operating activities' is simply gross profit less operating expenses and is another key performance indicator.

■ **Finance expenses.** Generally the interest cost of debt during the period. They are stated net of any interest received.

■ **Taxation expense.** The tax owed on the income/profit generated in the period.

■ **Net profit.** The bottom line profit (or loss) for the period after all expenses. It is either retained in the business or distributed to shareholders as dividends.

An illustrative (and simplified) income statement is shown below. Presentation may differ according to the type of business and associated accounting conventions.

Example income statement for a period ending on a particular date

	$
Revenue	110,750
Cost of sales	(65,500)
Gross profit	45,250
Operating expenses	(36,750)
Results from operating activities	8,500
Net finance expense	(900)
Taxation expense	(2,500)
Profit from continuing operations	5,100

An income statement summarizes total income generated and total expenditure incurred over a set period.

2.7

Understand the statement of cash flows

The statement of cash flows gives a full picture of a business alongside the balance sheet and income statement. It summarizes the different sources and uses of cash within a business and is a useful indicator of a business's liquidity and solvency.

■ **Profit versus cash.** In the long run profits should equate to cash generation, however in the short run a profit does not necessarily mean that a business has generated cash. As accounts are prepared on a matching (or accruals) basis, the timing of income and expenditure is not always the same as the timing of cash receipts and cash payments. The statement of cash flows fills this gap and measures actual cash inflows or outflows during a period from three activities – operating, investing and financing.

■ **Cash flows from operating activities.** Operating activities are the principal revenue generating activities of a business, such as sales to customers, purchases from suppliers and payments to employees. The cash flow is calculated by adjusting the profit for the period for timing differences, such as movements in inventory and any non-cash items (Secret 2.8). This is the key part of the statement of cash flows because cash generated from operations must pay for all cash outflows relating to other activities such as loan interest and dividends.

■ **Cash flows from investing activities.** The acquisition and disposal of long-term assets and other investments.

■ **Cash flows from financing activities.** Changes in equity or debt finance as well as dividends paid to shareholders.

An illustrative (and simplified) statement of cash flows is shown below.

Example statement of cash flows for a period ending on a particular date

	$
Cash flows from operating activities	
Profit for the period	8,500
Adjustments for timing differences	(1,650)
Interest and taxes paid	(3,250)
	3,600
Cash flows from investing activities	
Purchase of property	(9,450)
Proceeds from sale of equipment	2,250
Interest and dividends received	900
	(6,300)
Cash flows from financing activities	
Proceeds from issue of share capital	1,500
Proceeds from long-term borrowings	7,500
Dividends paid	(3,000)
	6,000
Net increase in cash and cash equivalents	3,300
Cash and cash equivalents at beginning of period	6,450
Cash and cash equivalents at end of period	9,750

This company has generated $3,600 cash from operating activities, despite making a profit of $8,500. The company has spent $6,300 on investing activities, which has been largely financed by $6,000 from financing activities. Overall cash has increased by $3,300.

The statement of cash flows summarizes the different sources and uses of cash within a business.

2.8

Watch out for non-cash costs

Non-cash costs explain some of the difference between profit and cash flow. This relates back to Secrets 2.2 and 2.7 where we learned that reported expenditure may not occur at the same time as related cash payments. The matching concept means that costs are accounted for when incurred rather than paid.

We will look at two examples of non-cash costs, being depreciation and amortization.

one minute wonder Does your business deal with capitalization of research and development? Where a product or service will definitely be sold, some accounting regulations allow the related R&D costs to be 'capitalized' i.e. added to the balance sheet as a long-term (intangible) asset. As a result, there is no immediate expense charged to the income state-ment. The asset or 'capitalized expenditure' is subsequently amortized over its useful life.

"Actually, if my business was legitimate, I would deduct a substantial percentage for depreciation of my body"

Xaviera Hollander, author of The Happy Hooker

■ **Depreciation.** Fixed or long-term assets (Secret 1.3) have a 'useful economic life' and reduce in value over time. For example, motor vehicles actually wear out and technology-related assets may become obsolete. Depreciation is a measure of how quickly these assets wear out over time. In Secret 2.5 we learned that a balance sheet includes the value of a business's long term assets. The majority of these values will be the original cost less any depreciation to date. In Secret 2.6 we learned that the income statement includes a business's overhead costs. These costs include depreciation, which is effectively a non-cash cost.

Therefore, a business does not recognize the full cost of a fixed asset in the income statement at the time of purchase. Instead the cost is added to the balance sheet and depreciation is charged to the income statement throughout the asset's life, to match its usage. Over an asset's life the full cost should be charged to the income statement, i.e. the cost is spread out over a number of years.

■ **Amortization.** Amortization is basically the same as depreciation, but for intangible assets (see Secret 1.3).

An income statement may include non-cash costs such as depreciation and amortization.

2.9

Be aware of account-ing regulation

An overview of accounting regulation is useful to help understand the context within which financial statements are produced. Most of the regulation applies to private or public limited companies as opposed to sole traders.

■ **Local and international standards.** Local company law governs the form and content of financial statements and requires companies to comply with applicable accounting standards. These standards provide a number of concepts or principles which underpin financial statements. They also deal with subjective areas which require judgement, for example property valuation. In addition to local laws and standards – the International Accounting Standards Board (IASB) attempts to improve and harmonize financial reporting across the world. The IASB

case study The European Union requires public companies to comply with IFRS, and many other nations have followed this lead, with the US as a notable exception. In 2002 the US government brought in new laws to restore public confidence after a number of

issue International Financial Reporting Standards (IFRS) which govern accounting treatments as well as the preparation and presentation of financial statements. Depending upon the size and type of a business it may comply with either local or international financial reporting standards.

■ **GAAP.** Generally Accepted Accounting Practice (GAAP) signifies all the rules, from whatever source (company law, local and international standards and other statutory requirements), which govern accounting. Most countries have their own GAAP – although, generally, local and international accounting standards are in the process of converging.

■ **Audit.** Companies above certain thresholds are required to have an external audit. An audit is an inspection of the accounting records and procedures of a business by an independent accountant, in order to form an opinion on the accuracy and completeness of the company's financial statements. Many large organizations also have an independent internal audit function as a separate department, which examines and evaluates business activities.

Accounting regulation gives consistency and comparability between different companies.

high-profile accounting scandals, involving Enron, WorldCom and Tyco, amongst others. The Sarbanes-Oxley Act, often referred to as Sarbox or SOX, sets out standards and regulations for all US public company boards, management and public accounting firms.

2.10

Know who uses financial statements

Financial statements are used for different purposes. The following stakeholders may be interested in the accounting information of a large public company.

■ **Shareholders.** Need financial results to assess the risk of and return on their investment. They will also want to judge how effectively management is running the business on their behalf.

■ **Financial analysts, advisers and journalists.** Will analyse financial statements for their clients and existing/potential investors.

■ **Credit referencing agencies.** Will use financial statements to rate a company's financial health and advise their clients, such as investors, providers of finance, suppliers and even customers.

■ **Providers of finance, such as banks.** Will assess the ability of a company to service and repay their loans.

case study Annual accounts are a key method of communication between businesses and their owners in countries such as the US and UK, where there are active and well-developed equity markets. In some European countries, debt finance provided by banks

■ **Suppliers.** Will assess the health of a company to predict if they will continue to make purchases in the future and more importantly are able to pay their debts.

■ **Customers.** Will judge the health and future direction of a company to predict if they will continue to be a reliable source of goods or services. Some will want to know how much profit has been made from their custom.

■ **Managers.** Will assess financial performance to help them make appropriate decisions. They should also have access to internal financial information.

■ **Employees.** Will want to assess financial health to ensure their future employment and remuneration are secure.

■ **Local tax authorities.** Will want to know how much profit has been made to assess any tax owed.

■ **Governments.** Will be interested in the impact on the overall economy, such as providing employment and contributing to gross domestic product (GDP). They will collate financial information to produce national statistics.

■ **The general public.** May be interested if a business impacts on their life and community. For example, the business's environmental, ethical and employment policies.

Financial statements need to meet the needs of a variety of people.

has historically been more popular. The banks have traditionally demanded more detailed and regular financial information than annual accounts. In these countries, government tax authorities have tended to be the main users of financial statements.

Making profit

The main objective of most businesses is to make a profit and in this chapter I'll explain how to make and increase profit. To understand how profit is made, you need to look at the different types of costs and in particular the relationship between costs, volume and profit. One of the challenges to most businesses is maintaining and increasing profit-ability, so I'll run through four established drivers that help to improve the bottom line.

3.1

Realize that not all 'costs' are the same

Detailed cost information is vital for meaningful interpretation of business performance and to enable costing decisions to be made that will improve profitability. Managers should understand how to allocate and identify different costs.

■ **Direct and indirect costs.** Direct costs can be identified within an individual product or service. Indirect costs are those that cannot be easily identified with a product or service, often termed 'overhead' costs.

■ **Cost behaviour: fixed and variable costs.** Costs behave differently when sales volume or production levels (hereafter, activity) change.

case study Kieran runs a wooden furniture business. His direct costs are the material cost of wood and the labour cost of his carpenter, who makes the furniture. His indirect costs are the rental of the workshop where the furniture is made and the power used to heat and light the workshop. These costs can only be allocated

"It's not what you pay a man, but what he costs you that counts"

Will Rogers, actor and comedian

The two most common costs are those which are directly variable with activity and those which are fixed and unresponsive to changes in activity. Note that fixed and variable costs can also be either direct or indirect costs.

■ **Cost behaviour: mixed costs.** In practice some costs include a mixture of fixed and variable components. A semi-variable cost includes both a fixed and variable element. For example, a typical telephone bill includes a fixed rental charge plus a charge for the minutes of telephone calls made. A semi-fixed (or stepped) cost increases at discrete activity levels. For example, to manage increased demand, a courier business may lease an additional vehicle once their existing fleet is at full capacity.

Understand the different types of costs for effective planning, decision-making and control.

to individual units of furniture by using estimations. Kieran's variable costs include the wood and power used in making furniture. His fixed costs include the rental of the workshop. His labour cost could be variable or fixed depending if his carpenter is paid by activity or by a fixed salary.

3.2

Know what is meant by 'profit'

Put simply, 'profit' is 'income' less 'costs'. However, whereas the definition of 'income' is fairly consistent, the definition of 'costs' can differ from person to person and country to country. Consequently, there are different and often conflicting measures of profit.

Even 'profit' has different names. Sometimes the terms 'earnings' or 'income' are used interchangeably for profit. When discussing profit with other people, it is wise to confirm which definition is being used. The most common definitions are outlined here.

■ **Gross profit.** The first measure of profit shown on an income statement. It is calculated by deducting 'cost of sales' from 'revenue'. 'Cost of sales' are the direct costs of sales, for example the wholesale cost of

case study EBITDA or 'earnings before interest, taxes, depreciation and amortization' (Secret 2.8) effectively cancels out some of the effects of accruals accounting (Secret 2.2), financing and taxation. Many debate its value and it is not formally shown on an income state-

purchases for a retailer. Therefore, gross profit is the direct profit of a business. See also gross margin (Secret 7.2).

■ **Operating profit.** The second measure of profit shown on an income statement. It is calculated by deducting indirect operating costs (such as distribution and administration) from gross profit. Operating profit is also known as results from operating activities or EBIT (earnings before interest and tax).

■ **Net profit.** Often referred to as 'the bottom line', as traditionally it was the bottom figure on an income statement. There are, however, differences in how net profit is calculated. The most common definitions are: profit before tax and after interest costs; and profit after tax and interest costs. See also net margin (Secret 7.2).

■ **Contribution.** The above measures of profit are derived from financial reporting, where distinctions are made between direct and indirect costs. For internal management purposes, using fixed and variable costs to calculate profit can provide a more useful measure. A key measure of profit for management accountants is 'contribution', which is calculated as revenue less variable costs (Secret 3.5). Fixed costs are deducted from contribution to arrive at 'net profit'.

Always be clear about which definition of 'profit' you are using.

ment. Nevertheless, it is widely used by investors as a performance measure and valuation tool. EBITDA was popular during the 'dot-com boom' because it ignored interest costs and allowed loss-making companies to show a 'profit'.

3.3

Differentiate mark-ups and margins

Businesses commonly use 'cost plus pricing' to set prices. 'Cost plus pricing' is where the price is calculated by adding a premium to direct costs to cover indirect costs and make a profit. This premium can be calculated by using either a 'mark-up' or 'margin'. There is sometimes confusion between these methods and which to use when.

Mark-ups and margins use the principle of gross profit (Secret 3.2), which is revenue less cost of sales. 'Cost of sales' includes only the direct costs of sales and excludes indirect costs (or overheads) such as administration, distribution, rent, utility costs etc.

■ **Mark-up.** Mark-up calculates profit as a percentage of direct costs. It is a simple method of pricing, as a premium is simply added to direct costs. The mark-up can be calculated as follows:

$$\frac{\text{gross profit}}{\text{cost of sales}} \times 100\% = \text{mark-up }\%$$

"Never ask a businessman how much percentage he puts on the price" Swami Raj, psychic

For example, using a 25% mark-up, a product costing $100 would be sold for $125. The gross profit on this product is $25.

$$\frac{\$25}{\$100} \quad x \quad 100\% \quad = \quad 25\% \text{ mark-up}$$

Mark-up measures the margin made on top of direct costs. It is useful when benchmarking.

■ **Margin.** Margin calculates profit as a percentage of sales price. Margin is like working backwards, as it enables a business to calculate how much profit is made from a sale. The margin can be calculated as follows:

$$\frac{\text{gross profit}}{\text{sales}} \quad x \quad 100\% \quad = \quad \text{margin } \%$$

Using the same example as above – a product that sells for $125 and has a gross profit of $25 effectively has a 20% gross margin. Therefore:

$$\frac{\$25}{\$125} \quad x \quad 100\% \quad = \quad 20\% \text{ margin}$$

Mark-up calculates profit as a percentage of direct costs. Margin calculates profit as a percentage of the price.

3.4

Consider the impact of discounting

Many businesses offer discounts with the goal of increasing sales volume and profits. Many assume that the additional sales volume will cover the cost of the discount. However, the impact of offering discounts on profits needs to be carefully considered.

See how to maintain profit levels with a discount

Let's use a simple example of a business that is considering offering a discount of 10% on a product that normally sells for $100 and has a gross profit margin of 30%. This means that the product has costs of $70 and contributes a profit of $30 per unit.

■ If the product normally generates sales of 100 units then total gross profit is $3,000 (being 100 units x $30).

■ A 10% discount with no increase in sales volume will reduce gross profit to $2,000 (being 100 units x $20). The lesson here is that reducing the price does not reduce costs, which are still $70 per unit! The discount has therefore reduced the profit per unit to $20 (being $90 - $70).

■ If the goal of the business is to maintain profit levels then sales volume will need to increase to 150 units to generate a total gross profit of $3,000 (being 150 x $20).

■ Therefore the business would need to increase sales volume by 50% simply to offset the impact of offering a 10% discount.

This impact is magnified with lower margins. For example a businesses with a 20% gross profit margin would need to increase sales volume by 100% to maintain profit levels.

Overall it should be noted that these percentages are required to maintain profit levels. If the strategy behind offering discounts is to increase sales (and ultimately profit), then the increases in sales volume would need to be even higher.

Calculate sales volume needed for different discounts

The following table illustrates the increase in sales volume required to offset the impact of offering different discounts on gross profit.

	Existing gross margin		
	20%	25%	30%
Discount	Increase in sales volume needed to maintain gross profit		
5%	33%	25%	20%
10%	100%	67%	50%
15%	300%	150%	100%

The lower the existing gross margin the higher the increase in sales volume needed to maintain gross profit. For example, a 15% discount on price on a product that makes a 20% gross margin requires a 300% (or three-fold) increase in sales volume to maintain profit.

Calculate the real cost of discounting and its impact on your profit.

3.5

Forecast costs, volumes and profit

Analysing the relationship between costs, volumes and profit at different activity levels is known as 'cost-volume-profit' (CVP) or 'break-even' analysis.

■ **Calculating 'contribution'.** Contribution (Secret 3.2) can be calculated in total or on a per unit basis, as follows:

> Contribution per unit = price per unit - variable costs per unit.
> Total contribution = revenue (price x volume) - total variable costs

The relationship between revenue, contribution and profit is:

	$
Revenue	X
Variable costs	(X)
Contribution	X
Fixed costs	(X)
Net profit	X

This relationship means that an increase in revenue leads to an increase in contribution. Also, as fixed costs are constant, net profit will increase directly as contribution increases. Knowledge of contribution is useful because it demonstrates the impact on profit from changing costs, prices or volume. This enables planning of different strategies.

"I would just about break even if I sold everything right now"

John Wayne, American actor and film producer

■ **The break-even point.** The break-even point (BEP) is the volume of sales, in units or revenue, where profit is equal to zero. It is the minimum level of sales to achieve, as anything lower will result in a loss. At the BEP, total revenue equals total costs and total contribution equals total fixed costs. This is useful to assess a business's current position and plan for the future. Using this principle, the BEP is calculated as follows:

$$\text{BEP (sales units)} = \frac{\text{fixed costs}}{\text{contribution per unit}}$$

Simple break-even example

Here is an example of a business selling saucepans, where the sales price per saucepan is $16 and the variable costs per saucepan are $8. Therefore contribution per saucepan is $8. The business's fixed costs are $100,000.

■ Break-even point

$$\text{BEP} = \frac{\$100,000}{\$8} = 12,500 \text{ saucepans}$$

Therefore, the business must sell at least 12,500 saucepans to break even and cover fixed costs. Sales above 12,500 saucepans will generate a profit.

■ Break-even revenue

Break-even revenue = 12,500 saucepans x $16 sales price = $200,000

Therefore, the business will need to generate at least $200,000 of revenue before it breaks even.

Use CVP analysis to forecast profit at different activity levels.

3.6

Know when to use CVP analysis

The concepts of contribution and break-even (see previous Secret) have many applications in planning and decision making. Here are some ways that CVP analysis can be used.

■ **Calculating a target profit.** A target profit can be a more useful target for businesses than the break-even point. By treating the target profit as an additional fixed cost, CVP can be used to calculate a target sales volume in terms of revenue or units.

■ **Calculating a margin of safety.** This is the extent to which sales may fall below budget, before the break-even point is reached. Essentially, it is a measure of risk and represents a cushion available to a business. It can be measured in units, revenue or as a percentage fall.

■ **Calculating the impact of changing sales price or costs.** For example, the amount by which prices would need to increase to maintain profit levels following an increase in costs.

■ **Optimizing marketing campaigns.** For example, calculating the amount of additional sales required to cover expenditure on advertising or a discount promotion.

■ **Rewarding salespeople.** Allows you to evaluate different methods of rewarding salespeople.

■ Planning new products and services. Lets you determine the optimum combination of price and volume for new products or services that will maximize contribution and thus profit.

■ Changing a range. You can calculate the impact of changing your mix of products or services on offer.

Application of break-even examples

Here is an example of a business selling saucepans, with a target of $50,000 profit. The sales price per saucepan is $16 and the variable costs per saucepan are $8. Therefore contribution per saucepan is $8. The business's fixed costs are $100,000.

■ Target profit. The business must sell 18,750 saucepans, or generate at least $300,000 of revenue, to cover fixed costs and reach its target profit of $50,000.

$$\text{Target units} = \frac{\$100,000 + \$50,000}{\$8} = 18,750 \text{ saucepans}$$

$$\text{Target revenue} = 18,750 \text{ saucepans x } \$16 \text{ price} = \$300,000$$

■ Margin of safety. These figures assume that budgeted sales are the same as the target profit.

Safety margin = 18,750 target saucepans - 12,500 break-even saucepans = 6,250 saucepans

$$\text{where BEP} = \frac{\$100,000}{\$8} = 12,500 \text{ saucepans}$$

This can be expressed as a percentage of the target:

$$\frac{6,250}{18,750} \text{ x } 100\% = 33\%$$

This means that sales could fall by a third before the business made a loss.

Focus on maximizing your contribution to maximize your profit.

3.7

Know how to manage profitability

There may be many types of businesses, but when it comes to managing profit there are four established drivers that help to improve the bottom line: increasing sales volume, increasing price, improving margins/contribution, and reducing fixed costs. They utilize the principles covered in this chapter.

1 **Increase sales volume.** Examples include increasing share of the existing market through discounting or marketing. Other ways are selling existing products to new markets, offering new products to existing customers and selling new products to new markets. The latter can be a high-risk but high-return strategy.

2 **Increase prices.** A $1 increase in the 'top line' goes directly to the 'bottom line'. Although increasing prices is one of the most effective strategies to increase profits, it is also one of the most difficult and uncompetitive. One way to do it is by differentiating, for example by investing in quality. Another is to charge different prices to different customer niches.

> **"If a man goes into business with only the idea of making money, the chances are he won't"**

Joyce Clyde Hall, founder of Hallmark Cards

3 **Improve margins/contribution.** This is a key focus for many businesses. You might reduce costs by renegotiating prices with suppliers or sourcing lower cost components. Simply changing the product mix to higher-margin products might achieve the desired effect. Sometimes it can be done by increasing productivity to generate more output from the same cost of inputs.

4 **Reduce fixed costs.** Many businesses cut assumed 'discretionary' costs such as travel, entertainment, research and product development costs. Whilst these costs may help to improve short-term profit, they often have long-term consequences that can have a disproportionate effect on long-term profitability. Other methods that help to reduce long-term fixed costs include investing in efficient administration, more effective staff utilization, optimizing use of power, negotiating cheaper leases/rents, and sourcing cheaper financing.

There is an obvious trade-off between some of these options. For example discounting to increase sales volume and increasing prices. The most effective combination of techniques will depend upon the nature of the business.

Volume, price, margin and fixed costs are crucial to your bottom line.

3.8

Be aware of tax

The inevitable consequence of running a business is that it is liable for tax on its profits as well as a range of other taxes. Tax is imposed by law and collected by government agencies such as the HMRC (Her Majesty's Revenue and Customs) in the UK and the IRS (Internal Revenue Service) in the US.

Taxation is a complex area and requires professional advice. This is only a brief overview, as tax is dependent upon business structure. The information here applies to limited companies.

■ **Income or corporate tax.** This is levied on profits. A company's taxable profit is usually calculated using different rules to the profit reported in its accounts.

■ **Employment (or payroll) tax.** Affects companies and employees. The company pays tax based on either the number of employees or their pay. Employees pay tax on their pay, which is effectively collected by the company on behalf of the tax agencies. This is often referred to as Pay-As-You-Earn (PAYE) or Pay-As-You-Go (PAYG) tax.

■ **Capital gains tax.** Levied on the profits made from the sale of long-term assets, such as property and other investments.

"Of two things you can be certain; death and taxes"

Benjamin Franklin, American philosopher

■ **Ecological taxes.** Levied by some countries on the environmental impact of businesses, such as emissions of carbon dioxide. They are often referred to as pollution, green or carbon taxes.

■ **Sales tax or value added tax (VAT).** An indirect tax levied on consumption of certain goods and services at the point of purchase. It is usually a percentage of the purchase price. The tax burden mostly falls on 'purchasers' and is usually collected by 'sellers' on behalf of the tax agencies.

■ **Excise tax or duty.** This is levied on the producers of certain goods, such as oil, alcohol and tobacco.

■ **Customs tax or duty.** Levied on importers of certain overseas goods brought into a country.

Tax avoidance or mitigation is the use of legal methods to reduce the amount of tax payable. This is usually achieved by claiming permissible tax deductions and tax credits.

A tax haven is a location where taxes rates are low or even non-existent. Some businesses are located in tax havens in order to reduce their tax liability. Examples include the British Virgin Islands, which has the largest number of offshore companies in the world.

Tax evasion is the illegal avoidance of taxes and carries substantial penalties. An example of tax evasion is deliberate misrepresentation of financial statistics to the tax agencies.

Understand the tax consequences of running a business in the country or countries in which you are operating.

Managing cash

Cash is the lifeblood of a business. Managing cash flow is essential for business health and survival. In this chapter I'll explain why cash is so important and why profit is not necessarily the same as cash flow. I'll explain the 'cash operating cycle' and run through some of the established techniques used by businesses to improve cash flow.

4.1

Understand why cash is king

The most common reason that businesses fail is not through lack of profit but through lack of cash. Many failed businesses are highly profitable but run out of cash.

■ **Profitability versus liquidity.** Whereas profitability is the return generated by a business, liquidity is the ability to pay expenses and debts as and when they fall due. Liquidity is essential for the financial stability of a business. A failure to manage liquidity may lead to a business being unable to pay its suppliers and debt holders, which may ultimately lead to bankruptcy.

■ **Cash is like oxygen.** A useful analogy is that profit is like food, whereas cash is like oxygen. The survival 'rule of threes' states that people can survive three weeks without food, three days without water, but only three minutes without oxygen. Similarly, a business can survive

case study Let's use the example of a premium car retailer, 'Sexy Sports Cars', which sells a low number of high-priced new vehicles, and a second-hand car retailer, 'Dodgy Motors', which sells many low-priced

"Turnover is vanity, profit is sanity, but cash is reality" **Anonymous**

without profit in the short term but cannot survive without cash. If employees and suppliers aren't paid the business will not survive for long.

■ **When the cash runs dry.** Although this sounds simple, many businesses don't place enough attention on their liquidity. Firstly, businesses aren't realistic when predicting their cash income and cash expenses. Generally, they overestimate income and underestimate expenses. Secondly, not enough businesses regularly forecast cash flow and foresee problems before they arise. When they run out of cash it's often too late.

■ **Ideal goals.** Naturally, both a healthy cash flow and high profits is an ideal goal, but in practice it is not that easy. The short-term goal of a business should be to manage cash flow, and the medium- to long-term goal to manage profitability.

■ **Deciding a suitable cash balance.** Businesses should discover their optimum balance of cash flow. There is a balance between holding enough cash to meet all short term demands and utilising cash in more profitable investments. There is thus a trade-off between holding sufficient liquid assets and investing in more profitable assets.

Successful businesses manage cash flow in the short term and profit in the medium to long term.

vehicles. The annual accounts of 'Sexy Sports Cars' show more profits than 'Dodgy Motors'. However, 'Dodgy Motors' usually has more liquid funds than 'Sexy Sports Cars'.

4.2

Avoid the overtrading trap

Many businesses strive for growth. There is a belief that fast growth is the best way to build a successful business. However, is rapid growth the best option for business with relatively low cash and limited access to new external finance?

Overtrading

'Overtrading' is an imbalance between the work a business receives and its capacity to do it. Overtrading is a symptom of fast-growing businesses, which chase sales and profitability at the expense of liquidity.

This is common in new businesses, which tend to offer long credit periods to customers in order to establish themselves in a new market. At the same time many suppliers offer only short credit periods (or insist on cash payments) as the new business has no track record. This gap between paying suppliers and receiving cash from customers is often financed via overdrafts. Eventually overtraded businesses enter a negative cycle where banks will not extend their overdraft any further. Growing interest costs and the associated debt means their financial status eventually reaches insolvency.

"Yesterday is a cancelled check. Today is cash on the line. Tomorrow is a promissory note"

Hank Stram, US Football coach

Overcapitalization

On the opposite end of the spectrum of overtrading is overcapitalization. An overcapitalized business has excess assets, which are not being utilized effectively. In essence it is not maximizing returns in relation to the size of its assets and in particular its cash. This is not so risky as overtrading but the money should be used to finance long-term projects or returned to shareholders.

Overcapitalization is often a symptom of a previously successful, mature businesses with minimal future growth prospects.

Finding the balance

It is difficult for a growing business to turn away sales, but success can kill a business as quickly as failure.

Controlled and managed growth is critical to the future of a business. Growth demands investment and only a certain level of growth can be financed by internally generated cash. Further growth requires external investment and there's only so much money shareholders will commit and banks will lend in the short term.

Success can kill a business as quickly as failure can.

4.3

Understand the cash operating cycle

The cash operating cycle is the length of time between paying out cash for inputs and receiving cash from sales. It is also referred to as the working capital cycle or cash conversion cycle.

Businesses should understand, measure, control and finance their cash operating cycle. It is also useful to be aware of the cash operating cycles of customers, suppliers and even competitors. The cash operating cycle is normally measured in days and is represented by the diagram below, using the example of a manufacturer.

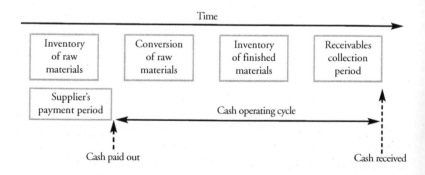

■ **Service businesses.** A consultancy working on long-term projects may have lots of money owed to them for 'unbilled work-in-progress' as well as long receivable collection periods. Their main input cost will be consultants, who have no payment period. A small consultancy business may have difficulty financing long cash operating cycles. As such, it is common practice for consultancies to ask for stage payments from their clients on a long project.

■ **Seasonable businesses.** Seasonal businesses, such as calendar and diary manufacturers have fluctuating operating cycles. Production is spread throughout the year and inventories will gradually build up. Trade receivables will increase from a low start as retailers stock up for the peak sales season, but may not pay until after the season. The supplier's payment period will be negligible and therefore seasonal manufacturers will require several months of financing.

■ **Retailers.** A large retailer such as a supermarket will have a relatively low finished goods inventory period (due to perishables) and minimal receivables as the majority of their sales are in cash. In addition, due to their size and purchasing power they can negotiate extended payment terms with suppliers. Therefore, some supermarkets will actually have a negative cash operating cycle, in that they receive cash from customers before they have to pay suppliers.

■ **The ideal cycle.** Businesses should aim to minimize their cash operating cycles. See Secrets 4.5 and 4.6 for tips on improving the cycle.

Know and try to minimize your cash operating cycle.

4.4

Measure the cash operating cycle

This section shows the method used to measure the length of the cash operating cycle (see previous Secret). This is used to assess a business's cash needs and any financing requirements.

Measuring the cycle

The following formulae can be used to measure the length of the cash operating cycle for a manufacturing business. The length is usually measured in days, although weeks or months can easily be calculated too.

Raw materials holding period $= \dfrac{\text{average raw materials inventory}}{\text{annual raw material usage}} \times 365 = \text{X}$

Materials conversion period $= \dfrac{\text{average work in progress inventory}}{\text{annual cost of sales}} \times 365 = \text{X}$

Finished goods inventory period $= \dfrac{\text{average finished goods inventory}}{\text{annual cost of sales}} \times 365 = \text{X}$

Receivables collection period $= \dfrac{\text{average receivables}}{\text{annual sales}} \times 365 = \text{X}$

Supplier's payment period $= \dfrac{\text{average trade payables}}{\text{annual purchases}} \times 365 = \text{(X)}$

$$\text{Length of cycle} \qquad \text{X}$$

Business growth, which will affect the cycle in the future, and seasonality, which will affect the cycle at different times of the year, should also be considered.

Financing the cycle

The length of the working capital cycle will help indicate how much working capital is required by the business and therefore how much needs to be financed. For most businesses there will be a proportion of their working capital requirement which is constant and a proportion which is variable.

It is advisable to fund the constant stable part with medium- to long-term finance. For the variable requirement, short-term flexible finance such as an overdraft is more suitable.

The value of investment required will increase over the cycle. For example, a business with 20 inventory days and 80 receivable days cannot be compared to a business with 80 inventory days and 20 receivable days. Although both have 100 days' requirement, the investment required in the first business is far higher, as the value of receivables (sales price) is more than the value of inventory (cost).

The cash operating cycle should be measured to determine working capital financing requirements.

4.5

Improve cash flow – 1

So far we have focused on understanding and measuring cash flow. The next step is to explore how businesses can improve cash flow. There are several sources of cash for a business. Here we look at generating cash from operations, capital expenditure and financing. See also Secret 4.6.

Generate cash from operations

Ways to increase cash income:
- Find new customers, especially those who are prepared to pay in cash.
- Offer incentives to existing customers to pay in cash (see also Secret 3.4 on discounting).

Ways to reduce cash costs:
- Review expenses for discretionary expenditure. Ask if items of expenditure, such as first class travel, are really needed. Can the business survive without them?
- Postpone expenditure – for example, use a web-based video conference instead of travelling to a meeting.
- Try to renegotiate large overheads, such as rent.

"It's easy to get a loan unless you need it"

Norman R. Augustine, US businessman

Generate cash from or reduce cash on capital expenditure

■ Consider delaying the purchase of new assets or extend the replacement cycle of existing assets, such as computers or motor vehicles.

■ Renegotiate the price and payment terms for unavoidable capital expenditure.

■ Consider leasing new assets or even selling and leasing back existing assets.

Generate cash from financing

■ Increasing, extending or rescheduling bank loans is a key source of cash for businesses. Banks will often demand assets as security and enforce strict covenants when issuing loans. The business will need to ensure it can cover interest payments from its cash flow.

■ Some businesses 'sell' or 'factor' their customer debts. Factoring companies will advance cash on outstanding invoices, depending upon the customer, credit terms and risk – for a charge. This can be an expensive form of finance, and – for small businesses – a trap, as once they start factoring debts it is difficult to break out of the cycle.

■ Shareholders may be willing to invest further finance into a business if they can foresee a return.

■ Alternatively, some businesses reduce dividend payments to shareholders in difficult times to keep cash within the business.

Operations, capital expenditure and financing are three key sources of cash.

4.6

Improve cash flow – 2

In the last Secret we looked at generating cash from operations, capital expenditure and financing. In this Secret we look at working capital. This is a measure of the operating efficiency and liquidity of a business.

Working capital is the difference between current assets and current liabilities. In other words the amount of cash required to finance inventory and trade receivables net of trade payables. Cash tied up in inventory or money owed by customers cannot be used to pay short-term obligations, and therefore businesses need to release cash from these sources where possible.

■ **Minimize inventory levels.** There are many methods of inventory management. A well known technique is JIT ('just-in-time'), used

case study Louis runs a picture agency and tried offering a 2% discount at contract stage for payment in 10 days, as opposed to 30 days. This approach had limited success. Some of his smaller customers, who were already prompt payers, took the discount and barely noticed the difference in cost. Many customers, especially the larger ones, agreed the discount and yet

mainly in manufacturing. Goods are produced only to meet customer demand. All inventory arrives from suppliers just in time for the next stage in the production process. This technique minimizes inventory levels.

■ **Minimize and control cash owed by customers.** It is important to follow procedures and be organized in collecting customer debts. See the next Secret for more on cash collection from customers.

■ **Maximize the payment period to suppliers.** Delaying payments to suppliers will not generate cash but it will delay its outflow. Many businesses use supplier credit as a source of finance. Large and powerful customers are often accused of dictating extended payment terms, which add pressure to a small business's cash flow. Extended credit should be negotiated as opposed to taken, to avoid problems in the future. Businesses rely on their suppliers to keep their operations flowing, so payment terms should always be agreed in advance.

Release working capital to pay short-term obligations.

still paid late! Louis realized that the 2% discount was not enough of an incentive, and that offering discounts to customers who were already late paying was being seen as desperation. Also, the cost to him was a massive 44% p.a. Now Louis only offers the discount to a few difficult big customers at the time of invoicing, and he uses an overdraft to help with cash flow.

4.7

Collect cash from customers

Ultimately a business generates cash from its customers. The question is, how long will it take them to pay? Some customers will pay quickly, others slowly and some maybe never. To collect cash from customers it is important to follow procedures and be organized in collecting debts.

The simplest way to avoid having money tied in customer debt is to insist that customers pay immediately for goods or services provided. However, to be competitive and attract customers, many businesses have no choice but to offer credit. Businesses that have to offer credit should follow these steps, where applicable:

one minute wonder Think like your customer. Look at the techniques used in your own business to maximize the time taken to pay your suppliers. You are your customer's supplier! Understand the rules of the game and play them to your own advantage.

> **"The payment of debts is necessary for social order. The non-payment is quite equally necessary for social order"** Simone Weil, French philosopher

■ **Check out the customer.** Use a credit referencing agency.

■ **Form an agreement.** Or even better a contract, which states payment terms. This could include receiving a deposit in advance.

■ **Confirm delivery.** Where relevant, businesses should issue a delivery note and get it authorized. It should be dated, referenced and contain as much detail as possible.

■ **Avoid part deliveries.** It is simpler for customers to match one delivery to one invoice.

■ **Invoice promptly.** Issue invoices with delivery or immediately afterwards, as customers will take credit from the date of invoice. Prompt invoicing also reduces the risk of disputes.

■ **Invoice clearly.** Include as many references as possible including order number, delivery note and customer contact. Include contact details and payment methods. State unambiguous payment terms.

■ **Follow through.** Ask for confirmation to check that invoices have been received. Eliminate the infamous "lost in the post" excuse.

■ **Be organized.** Maintain and regularly review a list of customer debts that clearly show 'days outstanding'. This facility is built into many accounting software packages.

■ **Keep on top of slow payers.** Maintain a set procedure for slow paying customers, which escalates after set time periods. For example, email, followed by phone call, then formal letter, then legal letter.

■ **Reduce the risk.** Consider credit insurance or outsourcing debt collection to professionals.

Cash owed by customers can cost you money to finance and is a liquidity risk.

Finance basics **secrets**

4.8

Prepare regular cash flow forecasts

A large number of businesses that fall into cash difficulties don't realize they are in trouble until it is too late. Producing a regular and frequent cash flow forecast is essential. It minimizes the cost of cash shortfalls and maximizes the benefits of cash surpluses.

A cash flow forecast should be produced regularly and frequently. They are most commonly produced monthly. However, where necessary some businesses produce weekly or even daily forecasts.

A four-month extract of a simple cash flow forecast is shown opposite. The aim is to show a net monthly cash flow and the resulting impact on the business's cash balance. The cash balance should correspond to the business bank account. Usually cash inflows and outflows are itemized.

"Happiness is a positive cash flow" **Fred Adler, financier**

Sample cash flow forecast

	January $	February $	March $	April $
Cash inflows	10,000	12,000	15,000	14,000
Cash outflows	(7,000)	(18,500)	(10,500)	(10,000)
Monthly net cash flow	3,000	(6,500)	4,500	4,000
Opening cash balance	1,000	4,000	(2,500)	2,000
Closing cash balance	4,000	(2,500)	2,000	6,000

In this simple example, January, March and April have positive closing cash balances, whereas February is forecasting an overdraft.

Cash flow forecasting enables businesses to make arrangements for shortfalls in advance. Banks will generally offer businesses more favourable arrangements for planned as opposed to unplanned overdrafts or loans. Similarly, businesses can forecast cash surpluses that can be invested in short-term deposits, where appropriate.

When producing a forecast, small businesses should be prudent. Income should be underestimated as customers don't always pay on time. Expenses should be overestimated in case of unexpected bills. The cash flow should always be a worst-case scenario. Cash flow forecasts should be frequently updated as events unfold.

A cash flow forecast allows businesses to predict and deal with problems before they arise.

Budgeting

A budget is a financial and operational business plan. In this chapter I'll run through the steps taken to prepare budgets and the major types of budget. Businesses invest a lot of time and resources in budgeting and I'll outline some alternative techniques which may help to improve budgeting. A key debate in budgeting is the level of participation and I'll explain the pros and cons of allowing wider participation in the process.

5.1

Understand budgets

Every year, most businesses will produce a budgeted balance sheet and income statement for the forthcoming 12 months. The budget should specify each asset, liability, income and expense item in detail.

Purpose of budgeting

■ Budgeting helps to integrate different activities. For example the sales department will need to communicate with the purchasing/production department about expected sales volumes.

■ Budgets are coordinated centrally to ensure the best allocation of limited resources across a business.

■ Budgeting allocates responsibility. There will be a number of budget holders who are allocated responsibility for part of the overall budget. Each budget holder will be aware of the business's goals and their contribution in working towards them.

case study Teresa is the finance director of a large publicly listed company. She knows that targets help to motivate the managers. At the same time she makes sures that budgets are a realistic expectation of outturn, especially when the budget is communicated

■ Setting motivating budget targets for each budget holder will help a business to control its direction and subsequently evaluate the performance of each budget holder.

■ For larger businesses the budget is used to communicate a forecast of future financial results to investors.

Levels of responsibility

Depending on the size of a business – budgets are divided up into budget centres, each with a budget holder who is responsible for setting and achieving the budget for their centre. There are several levels of responsibility for budget holders:

■ The majority of budget holders are cost centres and just manage costs.

■ Revenue centres, for example sales teams, are responsible for generating income.

■ Profit centres, for example retail outlets of a large organization, are responsible for both revenues and costs (essentially the income statement).

■ Investment centres, for example semi-autonomous divisions of a major corporation, are responsible for profit as well as assets and liabilities (essentially the balance sheet and the income statement).

Budgets are mainly used to plan for the future and as a benchmark against which to assess actual performance.

to investors. Her company's market valuations suffer if financial results are worse than expected. Therefore, Teresa creates two budgets: one which is communicated publicly and one which is used for internal target setting and performance measurement.

5.2

Follow the steps for preparing budgets

The 'limiting budget factor' prevents a business from progressing beyond a certain level. Determining this factor is the first step in preparing a budget. Typical limiting factors are maximum sales, access to finance, availability of suppliers or production capacity.

■ **Sales budget.** The sales budget is an estimation of revenue by product or service, typically itemized by product line (or service), price and volume. Sales budgets may be sub-divided by department or

one minute wonder Are you planning to draw up a budget using a spreadsheet template created by someone else? This can be a risky strategy because it may not factor in something that you need or it may have structural discrepancies that are not obvious at first. Another common problem is in using huge spreadsheet models – especially when linking sheets and using vast quantities of budget data. It is best to work from the ground up with spreadsheets.

> **"Before you can really start setting financial goals, you need to determine where you stand financially"** David Bach, American author

budget centre. This is often the first budget prepared, from which all other budgets follow, as sales are usually the limiting factor for most businesses.

■ **Production or purchasing budget.** This estimates the production or purchasing requirement needed to meet the sales budget, often sub-divided by budget centre. It will itemize the quantities and costs for each product or service and should link to the sales and inventory budgets. For manufacturers this budget will forecast production levels and when matched to capacity will show any shortfalls or excesses during the budget period. Any shortfalls can be avoided through overtime or subcontracting.

■ **Other expenditure budgets.** There will be a series of expenditure budgets such as administration, distribution, marketing, travel and entertainment, often divided into individual budget centres.

■ **Cash budget.** The cash budget (or cash flow forecast) is a forecast of future cash income and expenditure. The cash budget helps a business plan for cash surpluses or deficits and is covered in more detail in Secret 4.8.

The limiting budget factor determines the order of budget preparation.

5.3

Choose the best way to budget

A lot of businesses use traditional fixed and incremental budgets. However, rolling budgets and zero-based budgets (ZBB) can be better alternatives.

Rolling versus fixed budgets

Businesses typically prepare a 'fixed' budget for the forthcoming financial year. This process is repeated annually, and many businesses will use the previous year's budget plus or minus an additional amount for estimated growth or contraction. However, these fixed budgets present a problem when there are only a few months' visibility ahead.

Alternatively, rolling (or continuous) budgets are regularly updated by adding a further period (either a month or quarter) when the previous period has expired. This means that forward visibility is

case study Antony has successfully implemented ZBB on a cyclical basis throughout his soft drinks distribution company. On an annual basis a selection of his departments have the opportunity to zero base. This method spreads, over a number of years, the time

maintained because the budget always extends for at least 12 months ahead. Each update gives an opportunity to revise forecasts.

The biggest deterrent to using rolling budgets is the perceived time, effort and hence cost. This is why rolling budgets are less common than fixed period budgets. However, organizations using rolling budgets usually see significant advantages.

Zero-based versus incremental budgets

Incremental budgets are based on the previous period's budget plus or minus a percentage. These are appropriate where current operations are as efficient as possible. However, in practice, the majority of incremental budgets create inefficiencies that are perpetually carried forward.

An alternative is 'zero-based budgeting' (ZBB), where each budget holder prepares their budget from a zero base. Every item of expenditure (or income) in the budget should be justified and ranked in order of priority. Each budget holder is then allocated resources according to their priority. Budget holders do not automatically receive all their requests but will at least receive their top priority requests.

ZBB helps to identify and eliminate inefficiencies and wasteful expenditure. A disadvantage of ZBB is the administrative burden. Also, the prioritization process is subjective and difficult to ascertain.

Traditional fixed period and incremental budgets can be problematic.

and resources needed to practise ZBB effectively. This overcomes the major disadvantage of ZBB, being the time and resources needed. It also ensures that the whole of Antony's organization receives the benefit over three to five years.

5.4

Understand participative budgeting

'Top down' budgeting is where budgets are imposed by senior management. This ensures a strong correlation between strategic plans and the budget, and it is generally the quickest way to generate a budget. 'Bottom up' – or participative – budgeting uses input from those involved in day-to-day operations.

Participative budgeting can give more realistic figures and goals, and is more motivating than 'top down' budgeting. Those involved will generally feel more committed to achieving their budget.

Despite the advantages, there is significant time and resources required for participative budgeting. There are also unwanted side effects of participation.

■ **Budgets as an evaluation and reward tool.** Budgets make fantastic evaluation tools. They lend themselves to performance measurement. As a result senior managers have traditionally over-relied on budgets to measure performance. In addition, rewards such as bonuses or promotion are often attached to budgets as a sole performance measure. However, if budget holders are aware their performance

"Tell me how you will measure me, and I will tell you how I will behave" Dr Eliyahu Goldratt, Israeli author

is being measured this will affect their behaviour. There will be little incentive to set challenging targets that could drive the organization forward. There will be little motivation to do anything that does not contribute to the outcome of the budget, often to the detriment of the organization as a whole.

■ **Budgetary padding or slack.** This is where budget holders add contingency to their budgets to make sure they meet or beat their budget. This causes two problems. Firstly, in terms of resource planning, overestimated costs could lead the organization to become overcommitted with suppliers, and underestimated revenue may result in unsatisfied demand from customers. Secondly, slack leads to a 'use it or lose it' mentality where money is wasted on non-essential expenses. Under these conditions, achieving a budget target only means that costs have remained within accepted levels of inefficient spending.

■ **Competition amongst budget holders.** The status of having the largest budget is often said to cause excessive and inefficient budgets. Rather than creating efficiencies or eliminating unnecessary costs, some budget holders incorrectly believe that the size of their budget is linked to their status in the organization.

Be aware of the consequences of participative budgeting.

5.5

Calculate variances from budget

Actual results will inevitably differ from a budget. Accountants call the difference a variance. A variance can be favourable (better than budget) or adverse (worse than budget). You should monitor variances to measure performance and take corrective action where necessary.

■ **Meaningful variances.** To make variances meaningful it is inappropriate to compare the original budget directly with actual results. Instead the budget should be 'flexed' to take account of changes in budgeted activity. A 'flexed' budget is a budget which retains budgeted costs per unit but has been updated to reflect actual activity levels. It demonstrates what budgeted costs and revenues would be for the actual level of activity. Variances should be calculated between the flexed budget and the actual results.

■ **Flexed budget and variance example.** Rachel runs a purchasing department. Her original budget was $16,000. Actual purchases were $16,800, so on first inspection she appears to have overspent by $800. However, further investigation revealed that actual company sales were

1,200 units against an original budget of 1,000 units. Flexing the budget for actual activity shows that in fact there was a favourable variance of $2,400 as illustrated below:

	Original budget	Flexed budget	Actual results	Variance	
Sales units	1,000	1,200	1,200		
Purchasing dept. unit costs	$16	$16	$14		
Dept's total purchases	$16,000	$19,200	$16,800	$2,400	Favourable

Rachel therefore purchased more materials to fulfil the increased sales but at a lower cost per unit.

■ **Management by exception.** It is not usually feasible to examine every single variance from budget. Focusing only on variances above a pre-determined limit enables management to understand the most important variances.

One possible limit is to investigate all variance that are above a set percentage (say 5%) from budget. However, in practice a 5% variance from a small budget could be immaterial and not warrant an investigation. Likewise, 5% of a large item could be material and need investigating. Alternatively, using an absolute limit (say anything above $1,000) could mean that small variances which are a large percentage of a budget are missed. Therefore, it is appropriate to consider both relative and absolute variances. For example – variances over 5% and $1,000, with the additional caveat that any variance over 50% is investigated regardless of size.

Monitor significant variances between your budget and actual results.

5.6

Monitor budgets effectively

Many businesses have sophisticated budgeting systems, but they are ineffective because budgets are not properly monitored. Some simple changes can make a big difference to the overall process.

■ **Controllable and attributable factors.** Senior management will need to measure the performance of both budget holders and the area or 'department' for which they are responsible. Taking the example of a cost centre, the budget should be monitored as illustrated here:

Controllable costs	A
Non-controllable but attributable costs	B
Departmental costs	A+B
Non-attributable costs	C
Total costs	A+B+C

▨ A manager should be judged only on costs that are under their control (A).

▨ The department should be appraised on controllable plus any other attributable costs (A+B). Examples of non-controllable but attributable costs are the budget holder's salary and rent (if negotiated centrally).

▨ Total costs (A+B+C) will include non-attributable costs (C) and will be used for financial reporting purposes. Examples of non-attributable costs are allocated head office expenses.

"...and the failure was not my fault, but the fault of others"

Davy Crockett, 19th-century American folk hero

■ **Non-financial performance measures (NFPM).** NFPMs such as productivity, quality and customer feedback are needed to give a full picture of an organization's performance. Therefore, financial perform-ance measures, such as budgets, should be balanced with non-financial measures.

■ **Speed and frequency of reporting.** In a high-transaction, dynamic business environment, it is difficult to recall detailed events. Therefore, budget reports should be produced quickly after a period end and as frequently as possible. This will also make it easier to take any corrective action required.

■ **Forecasting.** Budget reports are often focused solely on the past. Businesses need information about the future as well as the past. There-fore forecast information should be included within budget reports.

■ **The importance of presentation.** The actual presentation of budget reports can make them easier to use and more accessible for budget holders.

Use these established methods to monitor and present your budgets.

one minute wonder Try a 'traffic light' system when monitoring your budget. The usual system is Green for Go: in line with budget; Amber for Pause: small variance from budget; Red for Stop: significant variance from budget, worth investigating!

Evaluating business opportunities

A business can be judged by the quality of its decisions. In this chapter I look at the decision-making process for investment opportunities. One challenge of operating a business is finding investment opportunities. Another is deciding whether to commit limited resources and money to these opportunities. There are a number of established financial cost benefit analysis tools to help with this.

6.1

Focus on the relevant costs

A financial cost benefit analysis should be undertaken when looking at a potential investment. Typical investment opportunities include projects (for example a new product launch) and capital investments (for example a new long-term asset). The concept of relevant cash flows is fundamental to all investment decisions.

Only relevant costs and revenues that are affected or can affect a decision should be included in the appraisal of an investment opportunity. The relevant financial consequences to evaluate are specifically the future, incremental cash flows arising from the opportunity being considered.

■ **Relevant cash flows.** As covered in Secret 2.7, short-term accounting profit is not the same as cash, mainly due to timing differences. Therefore only relevant cash flows should be used in investment appraisal. Non-cash items used to calculate accounting profit, for example depreciation, should be excluded.

■ **Incremental cash flows.** Only incremental cash flows (i.e. cash flows that will change as a result of the decision being made) should be used in investment appraisal.

Example 1: The incremental cost of using a salaried employee, who has spare capacity, on a potential opportunity, is zero. The employee is paid the same salary whether or not they work on the opportunity.

Example 2: If a business can sell a new product from its existing rented outlet, any share of the rent normally apportioned to products should be ignored for the purposes of the investment decision as the business's total rent bill is unchanged.

However, if a new outlet needs to be rented, then the additional rent is a relevant cash flow as it is incremental.

■ **Future cash flows.** Only future cash flows should be used in investment appraisal. Any past (or 'sunk') cash flows should be ignored as they are not incremental. For example, if a business undertakes research for a potential investment opportunity, the money spent on research is irrecoverable and should have no impact on the decision to invest as it is 'sunk'. Sunk costs include committed cash flows. A committed cash flow, such as a future commitment to pay for a past debt, will be incurred regardless of any decision taken now and therefore is excluded from any appraisal.

Make sure you understand which are the relevant costs and revenues when undertaking an investment appraisal.

6.2

Work out if an opportunity pays back

'Payback' is a simple technique used by many businesses to appraise investment opportunities, especially as an initial screening method. However, despite its advantages and natural appeal there are risks of using 'payback', and you should not rely on this technique alone.

Simply put – payback asks the question: "When do I get my money back?" For investment opportunities with a constant annual return, payback can be calculated quickly and easily. For example, an investment of $1 million that is forecast to generate net annual cash returns of $250,000 should pay back in four years.

For investment opportunities with variable annual returns, payback can be calculated by calculating cumulative annual cash flow. The payback point is reached when the cash flow turns from negative to positive. Businesses like this technique because:

■ It is quick and simple to calculate and therefore easy to understand. This is helpful when discussing the pros and cons of a potential investment opportunity.

■ It provides an intuitive measure of risk. The longer the payback period, the higher the risk,
■ It focuses on cash generation, which can be essential for the health of a business.

When using the payback technique you should be aware that total returns and cash flows after the payback period are not considered. For example, consider these hypothetical investments:

■ Investment A has 2 years of cash returns and reaches its 'payback' point at the end of year 2. Overall, it effectively breaks even (ignoring the time value of money).
■ Investment B has 10 years of cash returns and reaches its 'payback' point at the end of year 3. The subsequent 7 years of cash returns ensure a positive return over the life of the investment.

The payback technique would suggest that Investment A is better as it pays back quicker. However, Investment B has a higher overall return and may be a better choice.

■ What is the target? The payback is simply a measure and is not prescriptive. An acceptable payback period for one business may be different to another due to their respective financial positions.
■ The payback technique can be improved by considering the time value of money. We will consider this approach in Secret 6.4.

Use the payback technique for a rough idea of the value of an investment.

6.3

Calculate return on investment

A percentage yield or 'return on investment' (ROI) is one of the most popular measures of an investment opportunity, used by both business managers and investors. ROI expresses the profits from an investment as a percentage of its capital investment.

■ **Calculating ROI.** There are several different methods of calculating ROI. In its simplest format it is:

$$ROI \% = \frac{profit}{investment} \times 100\%$$

Where 'profit' is the profit from the investment opportunity and 'investment' is the capital investment required. Alternative measures use different definitions of 'profit' and 'investment'.

For example an investment opportunity which requires an upfront capital investment of $1,000,000 and is forecast to generate annual profits of $50,000, will have an ROI of 5% p.a.

A consistent measure should be used when comparing different investment opportunities.

"We know that there is a return on investment. Otherwise, we wouldn't be investing..."

Jim Sluzewski, spokesman for Macy's department store

Businesses like ROI because:
■ It is quick and simple to calculate.
■ It is easy to understand, especially as it is a relative (percentage) measure. This is helpful when discussing the pros and cons of a potential investment opportunity.
■ It is widely used by investors and analysts to appraise whole businesses. Using this technique to appraise individual investments will help a business to align itself with investors' goals.

When using ROI you should be aware that:
■ It uses accounting profits and not cash flows. The latter should be used to appraise investment opportunities in the most effective way.
■ The ROI percentage may be misleading when appraising investments of different sizes. For example, a 5% ROI on an investment of $1,000,000 may be better than a 10% ROI on an investment of $400,000.
■ The decision to accept an investment opportunity depends on whether or not the ROI exceeds a business's target. Setting a target ROI is subjective.
■ There is no one consistent measure of ROI. Therefore what is acceptable to one business may be unacceptable to another.
■ No account is taken of the timing of cash flows throughout the life of an investment opportunity. See also Secret 6.4.

Measuring ROI is popular, but don't rely on this method alone.

6.4

Understand the time value of money

Businesses invest in current opportunities in return for future cash flows. However, cash flows are worth more today then they will be in the future. This concept is known as the time value of money.

Firstly, let's ask the question: why is money worth more now to a business than in the future? Cash tied up in investments is a 'cost' to a business because of these factors:

■ The business could have earned interest on the money if it kept it in a bank account.

one minute wonder Use a simple spreadsheet formula to forecast future cash flows from an investment opportunity. Each future cash flow should be 'discounted' back to its present value. The whole investment opportunity can then be evaluated in present value terms. If all investments are stated in these terms then they can genuinely be compared on a like-for-like basis.

"The chief value of money lies in the fact that one lives in a world in which it is overestimated"

Henry Louis Mencken, American journalist

■ The business will be paying interest if it has to borrow the money for the investment.

■ Inflation erodes the value of future cash flows compared to their current value.

■ The business could have potentially earned higher returns from alternative investment opportunities.

■ Until the cash from the investment is actually received there is a risk that it may not be received, or less may be received than expected.

This cost is known as the 'cost of capital'. A good starting point to put a value on this cost is the level of return required by a business's investors, such as banks or shareholders.

Let's say the cost of capital (or return required by investors) is 10% per year. This means that $100 invested now should generate at least $10 a year and be worth $110 in a year's time, to satisfy investors. Looking at this another way, if the cost of capital is 10%, receiving $110 in a year's time is equivalent in monetary terms to receiving $100 now.

Accounting for the time value of money means essentially discounting future cash flows back to their equivalent present value i.e. what they are worth now versus the future.

Cash flows are worth more today then they are tomorrow.

6.5

Use NPV and IRR to appraise investments

The two leading investment appraisal techniques are 'net present value' (NPV) and 'internal rate of return' (IRR). Both use cash flows and utilize the time value of money concept.

■ **Net present value.** The following diagram illustrates the NPV technique. A typical investment opportunity consists of a cash outflow followed by a series of cash inflows.

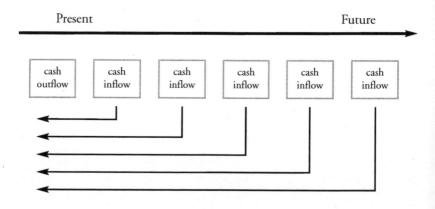

Each future cash inflow is 'discounted' back to its present value. Cash inflows and outflows are thus compared on a like-for-like basis.

If cash inflows exceed cash outflows, there is a positive NPV. As future cash flows are 'discounted' at a business's 'cost of capital' (see Secret 6.4), this means that an investment opportunity will exceed a business's required rate of return and is likely to be beneficial.

If cash outflows exceed cash inflows, there is a negative NPV. This means that an investment opportunity generates a lower return than that required by the investors and is unlikely to be beneficial.

To summarize: NPV equals the present value of cash inflows less the present value of cash outflows.

■ **Internal rate of return.** The IRR is calculated using a similar methodology to NPV. It is effectively a more accurate ROI (Secret 6.3) measure, which recognizes the time value of money and utilizes cash flows. The IRR produces a percentage return for an investment opportunity before financing costs. For example, if the IRR (or annual yield) of an investment opportunity is 15%, the investment will be profitable if the business can obtain finance at a cost of less than 15%.

NPV and IRR help you to rank and choose between different investments.

Measuring business performance

Business success can be measured using ratios. The majority of this chapter illustrates how financial performance ratios can facilitate performance measurement. In particular I look at profitability, short-term solvency and liquidity, long-term solvency and stability, and investor ratios. I complete the book by outlining the techniques used to estimate the value of a business.

7.1

Evaluate a business using ratios

Ratio analysis is a useful tool that is widely used to measure business performance. There are various groups of people who need information about the performance of a business. See Secret 2.10 for a list of these people and their needs.

Business success can be defined as "the achievement of business objectives". Measuring success will therefore depend on a business's objectives. For most businesses this is profit.

The financial performance ratios covered in the next few Secrets facilitate performance measurement between and within businesses. Note that such ratios are meaningless in isolation and should be assessed in relation to a comparator or benchmark, which could include:

■ the previous year
■ the budget (see chapter 5)
■ an internal division or department
■ a competitor

"It is much more difficult to measure non-performance than performance"

Harold S. Geneen, ex-president of ITT Industries

Care should be taken to compare like with like. There will be natural differences in ratios according to the nature of a business, its size, its age and the industry within which it operates. Additionally, the period of comparison should be considered. Ratios will usually fluctuate in the short term and therefore a medium- to long-term comparison period should be used.

■ **Limitations of ratios.** Ratios do not provide answers to every question and their interpretation can be subjective. They are a useful guideline to business performance but only a starting point for a full analysis. They are generally calculated on historic accounting information, which may itself include assumptions and estimates.

■ **Other indicators of success.** A variety of information will present the best overall picture of a business, such as other information included in a company's annual report (for public listed companies); the age and nature of a business; any recent changes in the business, such as new products or market; and any changes in the industry within which the business operates and the wider economy.

■ **Non-financial performance measures (NFPM).** These include market share, customer loyalty, productivity, quality, and investment in research and development. NFPMs should be used alongside financial performance measures to provide a balanced view of a business.

Know the uses and limitations of financial performance ratios.

7.2

Measure profitability

The business with the largest profit is not necessarily the best performer. Profit should be measured in relation to the size of the investment required to achieve that level of profit. Therefore, the best measure of profitability is 'return on investment'.

■ Measuring 'return'.

Gross profit margin (or sales margin):

$$\text{Gross profit margin \%} = \frac{\text{Gross profit}}{\text{Revenue}} \times 100\%$$

This measures the margin made on top of direct costs. A relatively high sales margin demonstrates the ability of a business either to charge a premium price or to control input costs. It is useful when benchmarking against similar businesses in the same industry.

Net profit margin:

$$\text{Net profit margin \%} = \frac{\text{Operating profit}}{\text{Revenue}} \times 100\%$$

This is similar to sales margin but takes account of operating expenses. Net profit margin measures the ability to control costs. Operating profit is preferred to other profit totals, as it excludes finance and taxation costs, which can vary between businesses and years.

■ Measuring 'investment'. The most common definition of 'investment' is 'capital employed', which is equity plus non-current liabilities (alternatively, total assets less current liabilities). Capital employed is effectively the amount invested in a business by both shareholders and debt holders.

$$\text{Asset turnover (times)} = \frac{\text{Annual revenue}}{\text{Capital employed}}$$

This shows how well the finance invested in a business, subsequently invested in assets, has been utilized to generate sales. It measures the amount of revenue earned from each $1 invested. Asset turnover demonstrates the number of times assets generate their value in terms of revenue each year. It is sometimes referred to as a measure of activity. A relatively high asset turnover could indicate efficient use of assets, although the measure is sensitive to the valuation of assets.

■ Measuring return on investment/capital employed. 'Return on Investment' (ROI) has many different permutations, the most common of which are return on capital employed (ROCE); return on net assets (RONA); return on total assets (ROTA); return on equity (ROE); and accounting rate of return (ARR). They are all essentially measuring the same thing – profit as a percentage of the investment required to achieve that profit. ROI is also used in internal investment appraisal – see Secret 6.3.

$$\text{ROCE} = \text{Net profit margin} \ \times \ \text{Asset turnover}$$

$$\text{ROCE} = \frac{\text{Operating profit}}{\text{Revenue}} \ \times \ \frac{\text{Revenue}}{\text{Capital employed}}$$

Analysing the net profit margin or asset turnover will help to explain a high or low ROCE.

Profit should be measured in relation to the amount of capital employed.

7.3

Measure short-term solvency and liquidity

Short-term solvency is the ability to meet short-term debts from liquid assets. Liquid assets include money on short-term deposit and trade receivables, but not inventories, which cannot be quickly turned into cash.

■ **Liquidity versus profitability.** As discussed in Secret 4.1, in the short term liquidity is more essential to financial stability than profitability. Cash generated from operating activities is a major source of liquid funds, as measured by the statement of cash flows (Secret 2.7). There may be other priorities for funds from operating activities, therefore it is important to have sufficient liquid assets to meet short-term debts.

■ **Cash flow.** The cash operating cycle is the length of time between paying out cash for inputs and receiving cash from sales (covered in secrets 4.3 & 4.4). It is a useful measure of the time taken to generate cash. Cash flow forecasts enable businesses to predict and deal with liquidity problems before they arise (covered in Secret 4.8). It is one of the most important measures of future solvency.

■ The current ratio.

$$\text{Current ratio} = \frac{\text{Current assets}}{\text{Current liabilities}}$$

This is a standard test of short-term solvency and simply measures if a business can meet its current liabilities from its current assets. Depending upon the nature of the business, the current ratio should usually be greater than 1, depending upon the speed of inventory turnover.

■ The quick ratio (or acid test ratio).

$$\text{Current ratio} = \frac{\text{Current assets less inventory}}{\text{Current liabilities}}$$

This is a more reliable short-term solvency measure because inventory is not easily convertible into cash for many businesses. This ratio should be close to 1, depending upon the business.

Interpreting low and high ratios

Don't interpret current and quick ratios too literally. Different businesses operate in different ways. Low ratios are not always indicative of insolvency risk and high ratios are not always healthy.

■ **Low ratios.** For example, a high volume retailer, such as a supermarket could have healthy liquidity but very low current and quick ratios. Supermarkets have relatively low inventories as their goods are mainly perishable and turnover quickly. They have minimal receivables as customers pay in cash. In addition, their purchasing power results in long trade payable payment periods. Therefore overall – relatively low current assets and relatively high current liabilities.

■ **High ratios.** A poorly managed business with slow-selling inventories and many outstanding receivables may have high current and quick ratios.

Short-term solvency is the ability to pay short-term debts from liquid assets.

7.4

Measure long-term solvency and stability

Long-term solvency ratios measure the risk faced by a business from its debt burden. Debt interest must be paid irrespective of cash generation or profits. Consequently, the amount of profit that can be reinvested in the business or paid as dividends is diluted. An excessive debt burden will restrict the ability of a business to raise further debt finance.

■ **The gearing ratio.** Gearing (or leverage) is a measure of a business's long-term financing arrangements (or capital structure). It is essentially the proportion of a business financed via debt compared to equity.

$$\text{Gearing ratio} = \frac{\text{Interest bearing debt - Cash}}{\text{Equity + (Interest bearing debt - Cash)}} \times 100\%$$

The ideal proportion is subject to the nature of a business and the current economic climate. In practice many businesses have gearing levels less than 50%. The higher the gearing, the greater the risks from dilution of earnings and sensitivity to changes in interest rates.

■ The debt ratio. This measures the ability of a business to meet its debts in the long term. It is a measure of 'security' for financiers. The ratio should certainly be less than 100% and many believe it should be less than 50%.

$$\text{Debt ratio} = \frac{\text{Total debts (current and non-current liabilities)}}{\text{Total assets (current and non-current assets)}} \times 100\%$$

The risk posed from high debt and gearing ratios can be mitigated by high interest cover.

■ Interest cover. This measures how many times a business can pay its interest charges (or finance expenses) from its operating profit (or profit before interest and tax). Ideally a business should be able to cover its interest at least two or more times.

$$\text{Interest cover (times)} = \frac{\text{Operating profit}}{\text{Finance expenses}}$$

The ability to service debt is a measure of risk to debt providers, shareholders and ultimately the business itself.

■ Net Debt to EBITDA. Although not a traditional measure of long-term solvency, the 'net debt to EBITDA' ratio has become increasingly popular with banks as a measure of gearing. (EBITDA stands for 'earnings before interest, taxes, depreciation and amortization'.)

$$\text{Net debt to EBITDA (times)} = \frac{\text{Interest bearing debt - Cash}}{\text{EBITDA}}$$

Banks will typically lend a business up to five times its earnings. Cash generated from operations (see Secret 2.7) can be substituted for EBITDA (see Secret 3.2).

Use gearing and debt ratios to calculate long-term risk levels.

7.5

Calculate investor ratios

Investor ratios are used by existing and potential investors of mostly publicly listed companies. They can be obtained or calculated where necessary from publicly available information.

■ **Earnings per share (EPS).** This is a popular profitability statistic used by financial analysts. 'Earnings available for distribution' is bottom-line net profit attributable to shareholders after all other costs have been deducted. Many remuneration packages are linked to EPS growth.

$$\text{EPS} = \frac{\text{Earnings available for distribution}}{\text{Number of shares in issue}}$$

■ **Price/earnings (P/E) ratio.** The P/E ratio applies to publicly listed companies and is a key measure of value for investors. A P/E ratio of 10 means that investors are willing to pay 10 times previous year's earnings for each share. Generally the higher the P/E ratio, the higher the growth prospects perceived by investors.

$$\text{P/E ratio} = \frac{\text{Share price}}{\text{EPS}}$$

■ **Dividend yield.** This measures cash paid to shareholders as dividends. This should be compared to capital growth, to measure the overall return to shareholders.

$$\text{Dividend yield} = \frac{\text{Dividend per share}}{\text{EPS}}$$

Mature businesses tend to have higher dividend yields than young businesses, as the latter reinvest most of their earnings. Investors looking for high-income investments choose high-dividend yield companies.

■ **Dividend cover.** This follows a similar principle to 'interest cover' (covered in Secret 7.4). It measures how many times a business can pay its dividends from its earnings. It is used a measure of dividend risk.

$$\text{Dividend cover} = \frac{\text{EPS}}{\text{Dividend per share}}$$

It also measures the proportion of profits retained in a business versus paid out as dividends. For example, a dividend cover of three times shows that a business has paid one third of its profits to shareholders and retained two thirds. Retained earnings are an important source of finance (see Secret 1.2) and therefore dividend cover is often high.

Use investor ratios to see if business goals are aligned with investor goals.

7.6

Estimate the value of a business

The ultimate measure of a business's cumulative success is its value. Valuing a business is an art, and there are a number of different techniques, which may produce different valuations for the same business.

■ Discounted cash flows (DCF).

Valuation = present value of estimated future cash flows

Arguably, this is the most accurate method of valuation, but it relies on access to information and the quality of the estimations used. See Secret 6.4 for an explanation of present value.

■ Income multiples.

Valuation = 'income' x multiple

Price/earnings (P/E) ratios (Secret 7.5) are valuation multiples for publicly listed companies. The long-term average P/E multiple for listed companies is around 15. This means that valuations are on average 15 times earnings (or profits). Note that P/E ratios vary widely with the economy and across companies, industries and countries. Unlisted business can use a reduced P/E ratio from a similar listed company, for an approximate valuation. The reduction should reflect the difference in selling private versus public company shares. Revenue multiples are an alternative to earnings multiples and use a price/sales ratio. They are useful for businesses with fluctuating profits or even losses, as revenue should be more stable.

■ Asset based valuations.

$$Valuation \ = \ net \ assets \ value$$

This method is a useful minimum benchmark of a business's value. The value of net assets in the balance sheet (Secret 2.5) is often based on historic costs, which do not fully reflect the future growth potential of a business.

■ **Valuing a business for sale.** Valuations are rarely the actual price paid by a buyer in the event of a business sale. The range of values are used by buyers and sellers of businesses simply as a starting point for negotiations. Other factors affecting value are as follows:

- ■ The strategic reasons for buying or selling
- ■ The number of competing buyers and sellers
- ■ The negotiation skills of both buyers and sellers
- ■ The state of the economy
- ■ If the purchase price is paid in cash or in shares
- ■ The views of different owners – if they all agree to the sale
- ■ If the valuation is for the whole or part of a business

Essentially, a business is worth what someone is willing to pay for it!

Jargon buster

Accrual
Goods or services received but not yet invoiced by the supplier.

Balance sheet
Or statement of financial position: report of a company's assets, liabilities and shareholder's equity at a given point in time. It shows what a company owns and owes.

Capital expenditure
Payments to purchase or improve long-term assets.

Contribution
Revenue less variable costs.

Creditors / payables
Amounts owed to suppliers who have offered credit.

Current assets
Assets that are help on a short-term basis within a business, usually for less than a year. They are either traded or 'liquid'.

Debtors / receivables
Amounts owed by customers.

Depreciation /amortization
A measure of how quickly long-term assets wear out over time. Depreciation relates to tangible assets. Amortization relates to intangible assets.

EBITDA
Earnings before interest, taxes, depreciation and amortization.

Fixed assets
Assets that are a 'fixed' item within a business, usually for more than a year. They are for continual use in a business. Also called long-term or non-current assets.

GAAP
Generally accepted accounting practice.

Going concern
An assumption that a business will continue in operation for the foreseeable future.

Goodwill
The difference between the purchase price of an asset and its actual value.

Gross profit
Revenue less cost of sales.

Income statement / P&L
Reports a company's income, expenses, and profits (or losses) over a period of time.

Intangible assets
Long-term, non-physical resources and rights owned by a business.

IRR / internal rate of return
A yield or 'return on investment', which recognizes the time value of money and utilizes cash flows.

Matching/accruals concept

Costs are accounted for when incurred and income when earned.

Materiality

An amount above which an item's omission or mis-statement would affect the view taken by a user of financial statements.

Net profit

The bottom-line profit (or loss) for an accounting period after all expenses.

NPV / net present value

The present value of cash inflows less the present value of cash outflows.

Operating profit

Gross profit less expenses / overheads

Prepayment

Payments for goods or services before they have been received.

Provision

An amount set aside for a known liability whose extent and timing cannot be precisely determined.

Prudence

Revenues and profits should only be recognized once their realization is reasonably certain. Conversely, liabilities are accounted for when they are foreseen.

Retained earnings / profits

Any unspent or non-distributed profits that are saved for future use.

Revenue / sales / turnover

Price per unit x volume.

Revenue expenditure

Expenses incurred in running a business, which do not specifically increase the value of long-term assets.

ROI

'Return on investment' or 'return/yield on investment'. Alternatives are 'return on capital employed' (ROCE) or 'accounting rate of return' (ARR).

Statement of cash flows

Reports how a company has raised funds and how it has spent and/or invested them over a period of time.

Statement of retained earnings

Or statement of shareholders' equity: explains the changes in a company's retained earnings over period of time. The statement essentially reconciles movements in retained earnings during the period.

Variance

The difference between actual results and budget.

Further reading

Alexander, David and Nobes, Prof Christopher *Financial Accounting: An International Introduction* (Financial Times/Prentice Hall, Edition 3, 2007) ISBN 978-0273709268

Anthony, Robert N. and Breitner, Leslie K. *Essentials of Accounting* (Pearson Education, Edition 9, 2007) ISBN 978-0132233538

Arnold, Glen *Corporate Financial Management* (Financial Times/Prentice Hall, Edition 3, 2005) ISBN 978-0273687269

Bhimani, Alnoor, with Horngren, Charles, Datar, Srikant and Foster, George *Management and Cost Accounting* (Financial Times/Prentice Hall, Edition 4, 2007) ISBN 978-1405888202

Brett, Michael *How to Figure Out Company Accounts* (Texere, 2003) ISBN 978-1587990335

Checkley, Keith *Cash Is Still King: The Survival Guide to Cash Flow Management* (Glenlake, 2007) ISBN 978-1888998771

Coyle, Brian *Cash Flow Control* (Global, Edition 25, 2001) ISBN 978-0852974476

Drury, Colin *Management and Cost Accounting* (Cengage Learning, Edition 7, 2007) ISBN 978-1844805662

Elliott, Barry and Elliott, Jamie *Financial Accounting and Reporting* (Financial Times/Prentice Hall, Edition 12, 2007) ISBN 978-0273712312

Fitzgerald, Ray *Business Finance for Managers: An Essential Guide to Planning, Control and Decision Making* (Kogan Page, Edition 3, 2002) ISBN 978-0749438500

Kemp, Sid *Budgeting for Managers: A Briefcase Book* (McGraw-Hill Contemporary, 2003) ISBN 978-0071391337

Maitland, Iain *Budgeting for Non-financial Managers* (Financial Times/Prentice Hall, Edition 3, 1999) ISBN 978-0273644941

McLaney, Eddie *Business Finance: Theory and Practice* (Financial Times/Prentice Hall, Edition 7, 2005) ISBN 978-0273702627

Moran, Kate *Investment Appraisal for Non-Financial Managers* (Financial Times/Prentice Hall, Edition 3, 2000) ISBN 978-0273644927

Parker, R.H. *Understanding Company Financial Statements* (Penguin, Edition 6, 2007) ISBN 978-0141032719

Pettinger, Richard *Investment Appraisal: A Managerial Approach* (Palgrave Macmillan, 2000) ISBN 978-0333800584

Ross, Stephen A., Westerfield, Randolph W. and Jaffe, Jeffrey *Modern Financial Management* (McGraw-Hill Higher Education, Edition 8, 2007) ISBN 978-0071286527

Shim, Jae K. and Siege, Joel G. *Budgeting Basics and Beyond* (John Wiley, Edition 2, 2005) ISBN 978-0471725022

Walsh, Ciaran *Key Management Ratios: Master the Management Metrics That Drive and Control Your Business* (Financial Times/Prentice Hall, Edition 4, 2005) ISBN 978-0273707318

Weetman, Prof Pauline *Financial and Management Accounting: An Introduction* (Financial Times/Prentice Hall, Edition 4, 2006) ISBN 978-0273703692

Chartered Institute of Management Accountants *CIMA Dictionary of Finance and Accounting: Over 5,000 Jargon-free Definitions of Key Financial Terms and Ratios* (Bloomsbury, 2003) ISBN 978-0747566892

Websites and resources

Warner, Stuart 'Budgeting in the Real World' – online course at www.FinancialFluency.co.uk (Nelson Croom, 2009)

Tailored Finance Training - www.Financial-Fluency.co.uk

Online financial jargon buster - www.FinancialJargon.co.uk

Online resource for finance basics - www.Finance101.co.uk

www.BusinessSecrets.net